the Ottoman
kitchen

Sarah Woodward

the Ottoman
kitchen

special photography Jan Baldwin

INTERLINK BOOKS

An imprint of Interlink Publishing Group, Inc.
New York • Northampton

First American edition published in 2002 by **INTERLINK BOOKS**
An imprint of Interlink Publishing Group, Inc., 99 Seventh Avenue, Brooklyn,
New York 11215 and 46 Crosby Street, Northampton, Massachusetts 01060
www.interlinkbooks.com

Text copyright © Sarah Woodward 2001
Special recipe photography copyright © Jan Baldwin 2001
Design and layout copyright © Conran Octopus 2001

Publishing director: Lorraine dickey **Commissioning editor**: Emma Clegg **Project manager**: Ann Kay
Senior editor: Katey Day **American editor**: Beverly LeBlanc **Creative director**: Leslie Harrington
Art editor: Vanessa Courtier **Picture research**: Liz Boyd **Production director**: Zoë Fawcett

Design assistant: Gina Hochstein **Food stylist**: Susie Theodorou **Stylist**: Roisin Nield
Proofreader and indexer: Michèle Clarke

ISBN 1-56656-412-3 (hardback)

Color origination by Sang Choy International, Singapore Printed and bound by Toppan in China

contents

Introduction

The feast starts with a bowl of soup thickened with eggs and lemon, just as it was served in ancient Byzantium. Some cold meze to follow — perhaps eggplant "caviar" from Syria, the flesh of roasted eggplant mixed with spices and olive oil; a dish of icy cold *caçik*, creamy yogurt flecked with cucumber and redolent of garlic; a little plate of goat cheese from Macedonia, with some fat black Kalamata olives on the side; fresh grape leaves from the Balkans, stuffed with rice and nuts; all accompanied by flat Arab bread sprinkled with sesame seeds. A few pastries: *sambousik* from the Lebanon, little golden bundles spilling out a filling of meat, pine nuts, and raisins, and *böreği* from Turkey, exquisitely light, watered pastry filled with melting cheese. A small pot of Circassian chicken with a thick garlic and walnut sauce and slices of eggplant fried in olive oil and dressed with yogurt, paprika, garlic and mint. Then a kabob of firm chunks of swordfish interspersed with bay leaves, grilled over charcoal, and served with pilaf rice delicately scented with saffron. To finish, a plate of cherries scattered over ice and a cup of thick Turkish coffee with a small square of baklava. Food fit for a sultan, but also food that can still be found today all around the shores of the eastern Mediterranean and its mountainous hinterland — thanks to the influence of the Ottomans.

A very brief history of the Ottomans

At the height of its glory in the sixteenth century, the Ottoman Empire spread east to west from Baghdad to Tripoli and north to south from Budapest to Cairo. Yet, despite their addiction to battle, the Ottomans did not invade in order to dominate — once they had conquered, they rarely sought to impose. Their empire never had a unifying language (nor, in its early days, did it even have a set time). Christians and Jews lived peacefully alongside the ruling Muslims. What the Ottomans were interested in was tribute — of people as well as of goods. Early on they demanded each family from the Balkans should give up a boy-child to come to the capital to be trained as a soldier: and so came about the elite corps of the janissaries.

The slaves of the palace harem were also from conquered lands, for no true-born Turkish woman could be enslaved. The mother of every sultan was a non-Muslim, non-Turk — a foreigner. And the first slave to achieve the ultimate objective of actually marrying a sultan (Roxelana, wife of Suleyman the Magnificent) was the daughter of a Russian orthodox priest, abducted by Tartars. It was in this way that the Ottoman Empire became a true melting pot of peoples and cultures — and of cooking.

Food was always honored by the Ottomans. In the early glory days of conquest they understood, well before Napoleon, that an army marches on its stomach. The ranks of the janissaries came from the kitchen: sergeants were from the soup kitchen, corporals head cooks or head water-carriers. The cauldron in which the one-pot meals or *firin* kabobs were cooked became the most precious item of all, to be protected in the same way as regimental colors. Loss of the cauldron might lead to the dismissal of the officers or even death by strangling with the bowstring wielded

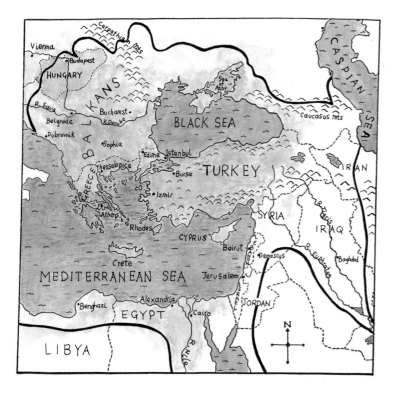

The Ottoman Empire in the seventeenth century

by the deaf mutes especially trained for the purpose. For slaves working in the great palace of Topkapi in Constantinople, to be appointed to the kitchens was an honor; to rise to chef a lifetime's ambition.

The fabled Byzantine capital of Constantinople (now Istanbul) was famous as the gateway to Asia, a city that straddled the divide between Europe and the Middle East. Under the Ottomans it lay at the very heart of the empire, and it was here that the treasures of the conquered lands came together. The Ottoman Empire

had a huge appetite and nowhere more so than in its capital, and in particular the palace or seraglio. Mid-seventeenth-century records suggest 250 tons of bread were baked there every day; 18,000 oxen were slaughtered a month; seven million sheep and lambs a year — and a tenth of all this went to the palace. A French traveler, Aubry de la Motraye, noted that the seraglio got through 100,000 pigeons alone in a year; a manuscript of 1660, listing deliveries to the palace storerooms, includes a note of the arrival of 2,000 pounds of cloves and nutmeg and 206 pounds of saffron. No doubt the spices were intended to flavor the fragrant pilafs that were the favorite food of the sultans.

To sustain this hunger, more than 2,000 ships a year sailed to the Golden Horn laden with foodstuffs. The Ottomans were not themselves keen traders (they tended to leave the actual business of trade to their conquered peoples, particularly the Ragusans, the Armenians and later the Jews expelled from Spain), but they certainly supported the principle of free trade. Many of their sorties were undertaken for the express purpose of seizing trade routes from their seaborne rivals, the Venetians. Once the Ottomans controlled the entire eastern Mediterranean basin, they set about obtaining the best foodstuffs from their empire and beyond. Every Ottoman city was a shopping center, and as early as the sixteenth century western travelers were writing of the glories of Ottoman markets. But nowhere was more glorious than the bazaars of Constantinople. The Grand Bazaar alone had 67 main streets and nearly 4,000 shops. You could find spices from the East, caviar from the Black Sea, butter from Moldavia, olives and dried fish from Greece, fruits and nuts from the Balkans, dates from Egypt, even live trout brought down from the rivers of Macedonia.

The cooks of the palace plundered the markets for exotic ingredients to produce ever more ambitious menus. The meals offered to exalted visitors were noted for their grand scale. The seventeenth-century Venetian ambassador Giorgio Battista Donado was shocked to find himself at a banquet of 130 courses. But if there was excess, there was also a true devotion to the sensual pleasures of the table and a continuing quest for the refinement of dishes. Poetry was written about the food, enjoyed in the idyllic surroundings of the palace with water tinkling in the background,

candles illuminating the tulips that symbolized the court, music lingering on the air. Later western visitors were to describe these feasts with awe, overwhelmed by the sheer style of the sultanate.

The Ottoman Empire was built quickly, only to decline slowly over the next three hundred years until its final death throes at the end of World War I. As the behavior of the sultans became more and more unsavory, with tales of caged heirs, fratricide, murder and madness within the palace, and the once

Iznik tiles, Topkapi Palace, Istanbul, Turkey

apparently unbeatable army lost sieges and battles, so the reputation of the Ottomans became tarnished. But in their glory years they maintained an empire remarkable not just for its scale but for its very cosmopolitan approach. The Ottomans were not afraid to take for their own the best of what they found from across the vast reaches of their empire. Nowhere is this more evident than in their food.

The Ottomans did not always invent the dishes that today have become classics of eastern Mediterranean cooking. Baklava came from Armenia, *avgolémono* has

a Byzantine origin, even the *böreği* or pastries for which the Turks have long been famous were modeled on the dumplings of Mongolia and China from whence the Turkic tribes came west. But if the Ottomans were culinary plunderers, they were also dedicated to the pleasures of the table, and in their palace kitchens they perfected the recipes gathered from across their empire. Some of the earliest exponents of fusion cooking, the Ottomans elaborated and refined the culinary traditions of the entire eastern Mediterranean region to create one of the world's greatest cuisines.

A few notes on my approach to Ottoman cooking — and the ingredients

I am no food historian and this is not a collection of recipes exactly as they would have been served in the palace kitchens at the time of the sultans. Where I have eaten similar dishes in lands that were once under Ottoman rule, from Syria and Lebanon to Greece and the Balkans, I have noted them, but I lay no great claim to authenticity, only to exploring a shared culinary tradition — one that I have sought to adapt to the demands of modern life.

Whenever I have mentioned Ottoman cooking to those who know it (usually via some fancy restaurant in Istanbul), they tend to remark upon its time-consuming nature. And it is true that the palace cooking sought to become ever more refined and therefore complicated. Personally, I have neither the time nor the inclination to hollow out a mackerel to stuff it with nuts, rice and spices, or bone a quail and then insert it into an eggplant — although these are both classic Ottoman

Lacquer-painted wooden panels in the Harem, Topkapi Palace, Istanbul, Turkey

dishes. Neither for that matter do I live the life of the peasant women of modern-day Turkey, who devote each fall to pickling and preserving, and the rest of the year to feeding their menfolk.

So in this book I have only chosen to include those recipes that I regard as both cookable and practical — as well as delicious. There are a few unusual ingredients, but only where they are vital (pomegranate molasses might be difficult to obtain, but it is well worth the effort).

Some things are better simply bought from a good supplier (Turkish delight being one, many pickles another). On the whole, though, the ingredients should be familiar, even if the approach to them may not be.

All recipes serve 4 unless otherwise stated.
All-purpose flour should be unsifted and spooned into the
cup measure.
For those concerned about possible health risks or allergies,
note that some recipes contain eggs that are not cooked through
fully, or nuts/nut derivatives.

an Ottoman breakfast

It is not unknown for soup to be eaten for breakfast, but, at least

in the hot summer months, a bowl of yogurt, a thick tranche of

comb honey and some rich fruit preserves made from figs, oranges and lemons are more likely. Not

that the savory element is forgotten — a pile of sweet black olives, some creamy feta cheese, juicy slices

of tomato and crisp slices of cucumber sprinkled with salt is a frequent offering. There will be bread,

of course, whether it be warm, flat, Arabic-style bread in Lebanon and Syria, or sweet, sesame-

sprinkled white slices in Greece and Turkey. And to wash it down, a glass of tea. We might think of

Turkish coffee, but black tea is the breakfast drink of choice in Turkey.

above *yogurt and honeycomb* **opposite** *olives, feta, tomatoes and cucumber*

Honey water

The addition of honeycomb to this delicate, golden-colored drink makes sure the honey stays in suspension in the water.

for a small jug *4 tablespoons runny honey; 1 tablespoon honeycomb; 21/4 cups boiling water*

method Pour the water over the honey and comb and stir well to mix. Leave to cool before straining through a cloth. Chill well before serving.

Beehives in southwest Turkey

Watermelon juice

Take a quarter of a small to medium-size watermelon (not vast) per person and remove all the seeds. Cut off the green rind. Put the flesh in a food processor with a couple of ice cubes and a few leaves of fresh mint, if available. You can also add a teaspoon of sugar per person if you want. Process quickly to a slushy consistency and serve.

Yogurt

Yogurt is a Turkish word, and there is a fanciful story that yogurt was first discovered by the Turks when the milk stored in camel bags on a caravan crossing the desert turned rancid in the heat and became yogurt with the rocking of the camel's movement. In fact, yogurt has a much older history, originating from northern Iran and spread by the Aryan races. It is even mentioned in the Bible as the Arabic *laban*.

Yogurt has always characterized eastern Mediterranean cooking. In the Balkans, a typical shepherd's snack remains a bowl of yogurt, a pile of olives and a hunk of bread; in Greece, yogurt sweetened with honey from Mount Hymettus is a favorite breakfast, while the Syrian breakfast often consists of *labneh* or strained yogurt, served with olives and flat bread. In Turkey, yogurt men may still be seen doing their rounds in the bazaars, tubs of that morning's yogurt hanging from a yoke across their shoulders. The creamiest yogurt is made from the milk of sheep and goats, always the prime herd animals of the Ottoman Empire.

Kurdish goatherd beneath a Syrian-Christian monastery, Mardin, Turkey

Yogurt drink

In Turkey and the Middle East, the yogurt drink *ayran* is popular with meat kabobs but I like it best served chilled for breakfast at the start of a hot day.

for 1 long, tall glass *thick, plain strained yogurt; iced water; ice cubes; salt; dried mint*

method Half fill the glass with thick yogurt and top up to two-thirds full with iced water. Stir well — it should have the consistency of thick cream. Add a couple of ice cubes, stir in a little salt, to taste, and a touch of dried mint. Leave to stand for 5 minutes — then drink.

Turkish tea

is traditionally served in small, tulip-shaped glasses with a rounded bowl at the bottom. The glass is placed on a saucer (often decorated with lurid flower patterns), together with two or three sugar lumps for you to add to taste. If your taste is Turkish, then the sweeter the better. The tea is always served without milk and strong and although the first glass may be at breakfast time, it is served throughout the day and late into the night. In the bazaars the tea-carriers are a familiar sight, swinging metal trays loaded with glasses at a seemingly impossible angle.

For the industrial quantities consumed in the bazaars, the tea is usually made in a samovar. To make it at home, warm a small teapot (preferably metal), add 3 teaspoons strong, black tea, top up with boiling water and leave to stand for 5 minutes. Pour from a height into small glasses (a few tea leaves don't matter), add sugar and drink as soon as you can bear to pick up the glass.

opposite from left *souk in Tripoli, Lebanon; tea-seller in Bursa, Turkey* **above** *tea-seller aboard a ferry on the Bosphorus, Istanbul, Turkey*

Sherbets

Although life in the Ottoman Empire was by no means teetotal (wine was the downfall of several sultans, such as Selim, known as the Sot), the drink of choice in the harem was sherbet, at least in summer. The first Ottoman capital of Bursa, from which the invaders from the plains once eyed up Constantinople across the Sea of Marmaris, is today a major industrial town. But it is still surrounded by orchards that yield an abundance of fruit, and on a clear day you can see the slopes of Uludağ, the mountain on which the city is set and from which snow was gathered to chill the drinks.

In the heat of summer, a sherbet-seller can still be found at the corner of most of the city's streets, offering fresh fruit sherbets to quench your thirst. Worries about the ice may make you resist when in Turkey, but back home exotic sherbets made from blackberry and rosehip syrups or pomegranate or watermelon juice make marvelous nonalcoholic drinks to offer guests — especially refreshing at breakfast.

Apricot nectar

for 4 glasses   *8oz dried apricots; 3 cups water; 2 tablespoons honey or to taste*

method   Cover the apricots with water and leave to soak overnight. The next day, drain and purée with the fresh water and honey. The texture should be very thick and pulpy. Chill before serving.

Pomegranate sherbet

for 1 tall glass   *2 or 3 ripe pomegranates, depending on size; 1 generous teaspoon clear honey, or to taste; iced water*

method   Either pick out the seeds from the pomegranates, taking care to leave the bitter white pith behind, and crush the fleshy seeds in a blender, or (my preferred approach) simply slice the fruits in half and use a traditional citrus hand-press, taking care not to press down too hard, to avoid bitterness. Pour the resulting pink juice into a glass. Swirl in the honey and top up with iced water. Crushed ice is also nice to add on a hot day, as is a sprig of mint.

soups and snacks
on the move

Soups were an essential part of Ottoman eating habits. The eating houses attached to mosque complexes, there to feed the poor, were known as soup kitchens; the elite corps of janissaries prized the soup cauldron above all other possessions. Soup has always been both a cheap and nourishing source of sustenance, and one that can be put together with just about any ingredients. But if the soups cooked up on the road were generally based on vegetables and grains with scraps of meat for flavor, those in the palaces and served at feasts became ever more fanciful; iced in summer, slaked with butter in winter.

Today no Turkish town is complete without its soup bar. The most popular is generally dedicated to tripe soup, to be eaten at the end of a long night of carousing, to ward off a hangover — not an approach I can recommend.

Soups fit for a wedding These soups

highlight the difference in eating habits between the

Ottoman court and the peasants they ruled over. The

almond soup derives from a nineteenth-century

wedding feast in Istanbul; over the page is a treat

traditionally served at weddings on the high plains of

central Anatolia. With its lacing of coconut, the almond

version is positively exotic, a light and fanciful concoc-

tion designed to show off expensive ingredients while

whetting the appetite. The wedding soup also aims

to impress, but this time through the inclusion of meat,

eggs and lemon — all rare commodities for the

peasant. Both achieve their aim, but it is probable

that what today is the peasants' version has the longer

history. But to start — a soup for the bride.

Bride's soup

Served before the wedding, this is a soup designed to give
the bride strength for the rigors (or joys) ahead.

serves 4 to 6 *3 white onions, about 13oz in total, peeled;*
1 large carrot, peeled; 3 tablespoons butter;
generous 1/2 cup fine-grain bulgur wheat;
3/4 cup red lentils; 2 tablespoons tomato paste;
salt and pepper; a blade of mace;
1 teaspoon dried mint;
1 teaspoon sweet paprika;
2 3/4 quarts water;
1 lemon, quartered, and fresh mint (optional), to serve

method Finely chop the onions and dice the carrot. Melt
the butter and sweat the onions and carrot for about 20
minutes, stirring occasionally, until tender and lightly
golden. Now add the bulgur and the lentils and stir well
so they are coated in the fat. Cook for about 1 minute,
stirring all the time, then add the tomato paste, generous
seasoning, the mace, dried mint, paprika and finally the
water. Bring to a boil, cover and leave to cook for about 45
minutes, until the lentils and bulgur are very tender (taste
to check — the exact cooking time will depend upon the
freshness of the lentils).

Check the seasoning and serve with the quarters of
lemon to squeeze into the soup and perhaps a sprinkling
of fresh mint.

previous pages left: *food stall, Istanbul, Turkey;* **right**: *Bride's Soup*

Village wedding festivities, western Turkey

Almond soup

12/3 quarts chicken stock;

7oz finely ground blanched almonds; 1 pomegranate;

2 tablespoons butter; 20 whole, blanched almonds;

11/2oz creamed coconut (Do not confuse this with coconut
cream, which is a thick, sweet liquid. Creamed coconut is
compressed into a bar, to be dissolved in liquid. Look
for it in the Asian food section of supermarkets,
or in Asian grocery stores.)

method Warm the stock and pour slowly into the ground almonds, stirring all the time. Heat slowly, continuing to stir, for 5 minutes, but do not boil. Take off the heat and let stand for an hour or so.

When you are nearly ready to serve the soup, pick out the pomegranate seeds. Melt the butter and briefly fry the whole almonds until golden brown. As soon as the almonds are cool enough to handle, chop them into small pieces and mix into the pomegranate seeds.

Reheat the soup slowly and check seasoning. (If the stock was sufficiently seasoned, it should not need any.) Grate the creamed coconut into the soup and continue stirring until it has melted. Ladle into bowls and sprinkle with the almond and pomegranate mixture before serving.

Women dance while the men gather elsewhere to drink — a village wedding in the mountains near the ancient city of Milas, western Turkey

Wedding soup

If you have eaten *avgolémono* soup in Greece you may recognize the flavors here — the principle of finishing with egg and lemon is the same. It just goes to show that there are no really good new ideas left in cooking: it is believed egg and lemon soup derives from the time when Constantinople was known as Byzantium.

*13/4 quarts strongly flavored lamb
    or chicken stock; 6 tablespoons butter;*
2 heaped tablespoons all-purpose flour;
5oz ground lamb;
3 extra-large egg yolks;
juice of 1 large lemon; 1 teaspoon paprika

method Bring the stock to a boil and turn down to a simmer. In a large soup pan, melt 4 tablespoons of the butter and stir in the flour. Cook over medium heat for 2 to 3 minutes, stirring all the time, until the mixture takes on a light brown color. Add the ground meat and cook for 1 minute longer, still stirring all the time. Now add a ladleful of the hot stock and stir well to amalgamate. Continue adding the stock, ladle by ladle, until you have used about half of it, by which time you can stir in the remainder all at once. Bring to a boil, turn down to a simmer and let simmer for 15 minutes or so.

When you are almost ready to serve the soup, beat the egg yolks and lemon juice together. Melt the remaining butter and stir in the paprika.

Check the seasoning of the soup, then draw off a ladle of the hot liquid and stir it into the egg and lemon mixture. Repeat the process, then tip the egg and lemon into the soup. Stir well and heat slowly, but on no account allow to boil after this stage or the soup will curdle. Spoon into bowls and pour a little of the butter and paprika mixture over the surface of each before serving.

note Typically for this soup, meat on the bone (such as shank of lamb) is boiled with vegetables to make the stock and then the shreds of meat picked off to add to the next stage. This works well if you are making stock in any case (and you can follow the same approach with a chicken as well as lamb), but for an altogether easier dish simply use stock (though from a bouillon powder rather than a cube) and add a little ground meat.

Pumpkin soup

2 white onions, peeled and finely chopped;
*3 tablespoons butter; 21/2lbs pumpkin or other squash,
    such as butternut or harlequin, including skin;*
2 teaspoons sugar;
1 teaspoon coarse sea salt; 1/2 teaspoon ground ginger;
1 teaspoon ground cinnamon;
1/2 teaspoon freshly ground black pepper;
21/4 cups whole milk; 41/2 cups water;
*a few fronds of fresh dill and freshly ground black
    pepper, to serve*

method Sweat the onions in the butter for 10 minutes until tender, but not golden. Meanwhile, peel the pumpkin or squash, removing any seeds, and roughly chop the flesh. When the onions are tender, add the pumpkin or squash to the pot, together with the sugar, salt and spices. Stir together and cook, stirring from time to time, for 10 minutes longer. Pour in the milk and water, bring to a boil, cover and leave to simmer actively for another 40 minutes or so until the pumpkin or squash is very tender. Check occasionally — depending on the nature of the squash, you might either need to remove the lid to reduce slightly or add a little more liquid.

Leave to cool slightly before puréeing — but not too much, because the soup should be fairly chunky. As with most soups, this one improves if left for an hour or so (or even overnight) for the flavors to meld. Serve sprinkled with a touch of fresh dill and a good grind of black pepper.

Cold yogurt soup with cucumber

The traditional hot yogurt soup is a substantial affair, but in recent years a diluted version of the yogurt and cucumber dip known as *caçik* has become popular on Turkey's vacation coastline — not surprisingly, as it is both cooling and refreshing on a hot summer's day. To make it, simply follow the *caçik* recipe on page 50 and dilute to the required consistency with iced water before serving the soup with ice cubes floating in the creamy white liquid.

Hot yogurt soup

Hot yogurt soup

In Anatolia, there is a popular spicy yogurt soup known as *tarhana*, made with a dried yogurt, pepper and tomato mixture that is melted into boiling water in a precursor of instant soups. Delicious, but not especially practical, given that you should dry the yogurt for several days in the sun. Universally popular, and easier to make at home, is hot yogurt soup. We might associate yogurt with summer, but this flour-and-egg enriched soup is a peasant winter classic. Do not omit the final swirl of butter and dried mint and on no account be tempted to use fresh mint instead.

41/2 cups well-flavored chicken or lamb stock;
1/4 cup basmati rice, rinsed and drained;
2 level tablespoons all-purpose flour, sifted; 2 egg yolks;
2 cups thick, creamy strained yogurt;
2 tablespoons butter; 1 heaping tablespoon dried mint

method Bring the stock to a boil, turn down to a simmer, and add the rice. Cover and let simmer for 20 minutes or so, until the rice is tender. Take off the heat and let cool for about 10 minutes.

Meanwhile, beat the flour and the egg yolks into the yogurt. Add a ladleful of the slightly cooled stock and stir well together; repeat the exercise.

Pour the yogurt and egg-and-flour mixture into the stock and rice and stir well. Return to the heat. When the soup is piping hot (but not boiling), quickly melt the butter and stir in the dried mint.

Pour the soup into serving bowls, making sure everyone gets some rice. Drizzle the mint and butter mixture over each portion and serve.

Meat ravioli with yogurt sauce

The Turkic-speaking people who migrated west with their horses across the upland plains brought with them the Mongolian delicacy of meat-filled dumplings. These were rough-and-ready affairs — twists of thickly rolled out pasta filled with a little meat, usually goat, then steamed or boiled and sauced with yogurt. Known as *manti*, this original food of the steppes has in recent years become popular as a snack in Turkish towns, as well as a staple in the countryside. The *manti* should be homemade and also very tiny — in the refined cooking of Istanbul they say you should be able to fit forty on a single spoon. But I find fresh tortellini are a very adequate substitute.

serves 2 as a generous snack
8oz fresh meat tortellini;
3 tablespoons unsalted butter;
3 fat cloves of garlic, peeled and finely chopped;
1 teaspoon paprika; 1 teaspoon dried mint;
4 tablespoons strained, puréed tomatoes (passata);
6 tablespoons thick, strained yogurt

method Cook the meat tortellini in plenty of salted water until it is al dente.

While the pasta is cooking, melt the butter over medium heat and add the garlic. When the garlic starts to sizzle, add the paprika, mint and tomatoes, together with a couple of tablespoons of water. Cook for 5 minutes, stirring regularly, until you have a thick tomato sauce.

Drain the pasta, spoon the yogurt over and then pour the hot tomato sauce over. Serve immediately.

Shepherd, Syria

Eggs cooked with yogurt

serves 2 as a generous snack
1 cup thick, strained yogurt;
1 teaspoon ground cumin; 1/2 teaspoon salt;
1/2 teaspoon freshly ground black pepper;
4 extra-large eggs; 6 tablespoons unsalted butter;
1 teaspoon paprika

method Beat together the yogurt with the cumin and seasonings. Fry the eggs in half the butter until the yolks are just set. Meanwhile, in a separate pan, melt the remaining butter and swirl in the paprika. Transfer 2 eggs per person to hot plates, spoon the yogurt over, followed by the paprika-stained butter. Eat immediately with hot bread to dip in the juices.

Eggs with peppers and tomatoes

I think of this dish, known as *menemen*, as the bus stop snack. Turkey boasts a very efficient fleet of buses, the preferred mode of public transportation in this vast country where twelve- to fourteen-hour journeys are considered short. For those changing buses, or simply waiting to get on, the terminals offer a wide range of snacks, one of the most popular of which is this dish of eggs cooked in a thick pepper and tomato sauce. I enjoyed it cooked to order in a little pan over a primus stove on a chilly morning as I was waiting to catch my bus — quite simply the best way to eat it.

The ferry terminal in Istanbul, Turkey

serves 2 *the bulb of 1 very large scallion or 1 small white onion; 2 small Turkish green peppers or 1 large green bell pepper; 2 long, green mild chili peppers; 2 tablespoons butter; 4 large tomatoes, about 11/4lbs in total; salt; a small handful of fresh flat-leaf parsley, leaves finely chopped; 4 large eggs; 1 teaspoon sweet paprika; red pepper flakes; 11/2oz feta cheese*

method Finely chop the whiter part of the onion. Seed both sets of peppers and cut the flesh into long, thin strips. Melt the butter, preferably in a pan you can transfer straight from the heat to the table: I find my copper *tarte tatin* dish ideal. Add the onion and peppers and cook over low heat for 10 minutes or so, until tender and just beginning to color.

Meanwhile, peel and seed the tomatoes and chop the flesh roughly. When the peppers and onion are ready, add the tomatoes to the pan, together with a generous pinch of salt and the parsley. Cook, stirring a few times, for 10 minutes or so, until the tomatoes break down and you have a thick mixture that covers the bottom of the pan.

At this stage you can leave the vegetable mixture until you are ready to eat (which is what they do at the bus stands). Just before serving, put the pan over medium heat. Make 4 small holes in the surface of the sauce, one in each corner, and carefully break an egg into each. Cover and leave to cook for 3 to 4 minutes, until the eggs are just set (tilt the pan to see whether the white runs). Sprinkle the paprika and red pepper flakes to taste over the eggs, crumble the feta over as well and serve immediately — with lots of bread, preferably flat, to dip in the egg yolks and sauce.

Pasta with parsley, cheese and walnuts

For centuries the Genoese played an important role in Istanbul life, and this country dish of rough pasta sauced with cheese, herbs and nuts is in some ways reminiscent of the classic Genoese sauce, pesto — except the constituent parts are left separate rather than pounded together. But then again, similar dishes are found in the hills of mainland Greece. Whatever its origins, it is very good.

Pasta drying in the sun, Kars, eastern Turkey

21/2 to 3oz dried pasta per person (see note below);
31/2oz skinned walnuts, roughly chopped;
a generous bunch of fresh flat-leaf parsley, stems removed
*   and leaves roughly chopped;*
31/2oz halloumi cheese, grated (for a slightly less
*   salty effect, substitute Parmesan);*
2oz feta cheese, drained and crumbled;
3 tablespoons unsalted butter;
1 teaspoon red pepper flakes (or less, to taste)

method   Heat the oven to 350°F and place an earthenware or other similar heatproof dish in it.

Bring a large pan of salted water to a boil and cook the pasta according to the directions on the package. Meanwhile, mix together the walnuts, parsley and halloumi (or Parmesan) and feta cheeses.

When the pasta is not quite al dente (taste to check), drain and transfer to the warm serving dish. Toss in the butter and then stir in the nut, parsley and cheese mixture. Return to the heated oven for 5 minutes before sprinkling with the red pepper flakes and serving immediately.

note   In Turkey and Greece this is traditionally made with twists of homemade pasta. I find the dried Genoese *trofie* or the southern Italian *fricielli* the best substitutes. At a pinch you can also use small penne or macaroni.

Beans in tomato sauce

It is easy to forget that much of Turkey is cold for much of the year. For a rapid warmup, you cannot beat a bowl of beans simmered in tomato sauce, bought from a street vendor or in a small *lokanta* or eating house.

1 1/3 cups dried borlotti beans, soaked in water overnight;
6 tablespoons olive oil;
4 small white onions, peeled and finely chopped;
6 cloves of garlic, peeled and crushed;
5 tomatoes, about 1lb in total, peeled,
    seeded and roughly chopped;
2 teaspoons sugar; 1 teaspoon paprika;
a good pinch of red pepper flakes; a good pinch of dried dill;
a handful of fresh flat-leaf parsley, chopped;
1 cup water; sea salt and freshly ground
    black pepper

method   Bring a large pan of unsalted water to a boil (salting it will toughen the beans) and boil the beans, uncovered, for 30 to 40 minutes, until tender (the exact cooking time will depend upon their freshness). Meanwhile, heat the oil in a heavy Dutch oven and fry the onions and garlic, stirring occasionally, until golden — about 20 minutes.

When the beans are tender, drain them and set aside. Add the tomato, sugar, paprika and red pepper flakes to the onion mixture and cook, stirring from time to time, for 5 minutes. Now stir in the drained beans, add the dill and parsley (you can reserve a little to sprinkle over the top when serving) and stir all well together. Add the water, cover and leave to cook for 45 minutes or so. Check occasionally — you might need to add a little more water, but not too much, because the mixture should be reasonably dry. Season to taste. The beans can be eaten hot or cold, and are at their best an hour or two after cooking.

note   The beans are traditionally served as a healthy meal in themselves with yogurt and flat bread.

Dried beans for sale in the Egyptian Bazaar, Istanbul, Turkey

from the meze table

The serving of meze, that selection of tasty morsels that precedes the main course of grilled or broiled meats or fish, is today a habit all over the eastern Mediterranean as well as in the Middle East. According to food scholar Alan Davidson, this may be where the very word derives from, after the Persian word *maza*, for "taste or relish." And in his *Oxford Companion to Food* he quotes Ayla Agar as linking the origins of meze to the enjoyment of wine in ancient Persia.

Apparently the original meze were likely to have been "tart fruits, such as pomegranates, quinces and citrons, designed to alleviate the bitter taste left by unripe wine." Fortunately, although the link between meze and drinking remains strong, the dishes themselves have moved on a long way. Today some of the most delicious of foods can be found at this stage of the meal.

opposite *food stall, Bursa, Turkey* **above from left** *Hot Crushed Tomato Paste (p42), Eggplant Salad (p49), Bulgur Wheat Salad (p46)*

Istanbul still has a few of the infamous *meyhanes* or drinking dens in the cosmopolitan Galata district, where once spies and embassy staff gathered to swap gossip over glasses of *raki*, the aniseed-flavored spirit that is the drink of choice. Come in for a drink and you will be offered little plates of delicacies to help absorb the alcohol. Moving from olives and pickles through cold purées of vegetables to little bowls of fried fish and spiced meats, you can easily spin a whole meal out of meze.

Even if the alcohol is not, this slow, measured approach to eating, with lots of small dishes, is very much in the Ottoman tradition, when banquets could feature hundreds of offerings. You will find many of the same meze dishes in Greece, Syria, Egypt and the Lebanon; in the Balkans the habit of eating pickles with drinks remains, although the dishes differ. Perhaps that is because most meze dishes are ideally consumed on a hot summer's day.

The aim in eating meze is to achieve a balance. First, of textures: a smooth vegetable purée, a crisp lettuce leaf, a chewy mouthful of herbs and bulgur wheat. Then of temperatures: an icy cold garlic and yogurt dip, a piping hot pastry, a tepid stuffed bell pepper. And finally, of course, of flavors: a sweet-and-mild zucchini fritter, a nutty potted chicken sharp with cilantro, a spicy mouthful of lamb's liver. The point is to mix and match.

Sharing meze, Turkey

Albanian liver

Albania fell to the Ottomans shortly after Serbia and Bosnia, in the mid-fifteenth century, and the Albanians were soon to become an integral element of the shifting population of the empire, playing a particular role in the army and the construction industry — their specialization was the building of aqueducts. This dish of lamb's liver cooked with paprika and garlic soon became an Ottoman favorite that lives on in Turkish, Greek and Middle Eastern food today. It is one of the few recipes that still acknowledges its country of origin — wherever it is found, it is called Albanian liver. The accompanying onion and parsley salad, flavored with sumac, is vital for both flavor and texture.

1lb lamb's liver; sea salt;
1 heaped teaspoon paprika; a good pinch of red pepper flakes;
1 large white onion, peeled;
1 teaspoon sumac;
a good handful of fresh flat-leaf parsley,
    leaves finely chopped;
olive oil; all-purpose flour; freshly ground black pepper;
1 lemon, quartered, to serve

method Rinse the liver well, then trim it of any membrane and gristle, and cut into bite-size pieces. Sprinkle it generously with salt, add the paprika and red pepper flakes and leave to stand for 30 minutes or so.

Meanwhile, cut the onion in half and slice into fine half-moons. Sprinkle the onion with 2 teaspoons of salt and let stand for 10 minutes. Rinse it well under running water then drain thoroughly, squeezing with your hands to get rid of excess moisture. Add the sumac and parsley and pile on one half of a serving plate.

When you are nearly ready to eat, heat 4 tablespoons of olive oil in a heavy skillet over medium heat. Sprinkle some flour over the countertop or a wooden chopping board and add plenty of pepper. Lightly roll the liver pieces in the flour, shaking them to get rid of any excess.

The oil is hot enough when a piece of liver placed in the pan begins to sizzle immediately. Fry the liver in several batches, stirring all the time — it needs no more than a couple of minutes at most or it will toughen. Lift each batch of liver out with a draining spoon and, if necessary, add a little more oil to the pan before frying the next batch — but make sure the oil is hot enough before you add the liver.

Pile all the liver onto the other half of the serving plate, add the quarters of lemon and serve immediately. The trick is to have a mouthful of tender, spicy liver followed by a little of the onion and parsley salad.

Kibbeh nayé

Kibbeh may be the national dish of the Lebanon, but versions of this mixture of pounded meat and bulgur wheat are also found in Greece, Turkey and the Balkans. Cooked *kibbeh* usually involves a crisp outer kernel encasing a spiced lamb and nut mixture — delicious, but definitely an art form. But in this Lebanese version of steak tartare, there is less artifice and more reliance on the purest of ingredients — raw lamb, crushed to a pulp with a little soaked bulgur, dressed with the finest olive oil and served with fresh mint, sliced red onion and a touch of chili. You must trust your butcher for this dish; I recommend you use organically reared lamb, and it should have a little fat about it.

The point of *kibbeh nayé* is the smooth, elastic texture of the raw meat. Traditionally this is achieved by lengthy pounding with a pestle in a large mortar, and in traditional villages of the Lebanese highlands the death of a family member is marked by inverting the mortar for a month. Luckily good (and much more rapid) results can be achieved with a food processor.

1lb very fresh ground lamb from the leg;
sea salt and freshly ground black pepper;
1/2 cup fine bulgur wheat; 2 or 3 ice cubes;
extra-virgin olive oil; a small bunch of fresh mint;
1 large red onion, peeled and sliced into fine half moons;
cayenne pepper, to taste

method Season the meat generously. Pour a little boiling water over the bulgur wheat (enough to barely cover) and leave to stand for 10 minutes, until the grains swell. Process the meat and wheat together to a smooth paste, adding the ice cubes as necessary to "relax" the meat. Spread the resulting paste on a chilled plate and serve with a jug of olive oil, some fresh mint leaves, the onion and the cayenne pepper, so diners can dress the meat to their satisfaction.

Circassian chicken

The Circassian women in the harem of the palace had a reputation as great beauties and good cooks, and perhaps it was one of them who first brought this Georgian recipe to Constantinople. One observer describes women picking apart the chicken "hair by hair" and then packing it in a vast pot with the ground walnuts and leaving it overnight before turning it out. You don't have to go to such lengths.

7oz cooked chicken breast or leg, skin removed;
3 thick slices of white bread, crusts removed;
1 cup shelled walnuts (pieces are fine);
1 heaped teaspoon cumin seeds; 2 fat cloves of garlic, peeled;
a good pinch of sea salt; 2 to 4 tablespoons chicken stock;
2 tablespoons finely chopped fresh cilantro leaves;
a good pinch of paprika; freshly ground black pepper;

method With a fork, shred the chicken. Soak the bread in a little water. Heat a heavy-bottomed skillet over medium heat and briefly (a minute or so, stirring) toast the walnuts and cumin seeds, taking care that they do not burn. In a food processor or with a mortar and pestle, crush the walnuts and cumin seeds with the garlic and salt. Aim for a knobbly mixture rather than a smooth paste.

Gently warm the stock. Squeeze the bread dry and add the walnut mixture, together with 2 tablespoons of the warm stock. Either pound together to amalgamate or return to the processor — I think the former method gives the better texture, which, again, should be knobbly rather than smooth. Add more stock if necessary, but make sure the mixture does not become too wet. Mix in the cilantro leaves, reserving a little for a garnish, and add the paprika and a generous grinding of black pepper. Finally, stir in the shredded chicken.

Line 4 small ramekins with plastic wrap, letting it hang over the edge, spoon in the chicken and walnut mixture, pressing it down hard. Chill the ramekins in the refrigerator for several hours before turning out and serving.

Beans with sesame

This dish comes from Antalya on Turkey's southern coast, but in its use of tahini or sesame paste it bears strong similarities to dishes found over the border in Syria.

1lb canned cannellini beans;
1 clove of garlic, peeled and minced; juice of 1 large lemon;
a good pinch of sea salt;
2 tablespoons sour grape juice or, failing that,
    1 tablespoon red-wine vinegar;
2 tablespoons light tahini sauce, drained of oil;
1 to 2 tablespoons water;
1 tablespoon finely chopped fresh flat-leaf parsley;
1 tablespoon pine nuts; 1 teaspoon cumin seeds;
1 teaspoon paprika; 2 tablespoons extra-virgin olive oil

method   Drain the beans, rinse well and place in a heavy bottomed pan. Mix together the garlic, lemon juice, salt and grape juice or red-wine vinegar. Beat this mixture into the tahini, together with the water — just enough to slacken the mixture. Pour over the beans and place the pot over low heat. Warm slowly for 2 to 3 minutes, stirring, but being careful not to break up the beans: do not let boil or the mixture can split.

Pour the dressed beans into a serving dish and stir in the chopped parsley. Let stand for several hours.

Just before you are ready to eat, heat a heavy-bottomed, dry skillet and briefly (1 or 2 minutes, stirring) toast the pine nuts, being careful that they do not burn. Then toast the cumin seeds for 30 seconds. Sprinkle both over the beans. Whisk the paprika into the olive oil and then pour over the surface of the beans.

Sifting sesame seeds, Patara, Turkey

Cheese with mushrooms

The finest cooks in the Ottoman Empire were reputed to come from Bolu, east of Istanbul on the central Anatolian plain. Although it is now an alarmingly polluted industrial town, Bolu remains surrounded by luxuriantly wooded hillsides where wild mushrooms grow abundantly.

It was a cook from Bolu, working in a restaurant opposite Istanbul's extraordinary Byzantine church of St. Saviour in Chora, who served me this simple, but exquisite, dish. The cheese he used was smoked and described as Circassian — you can use the salty halloumi.

8oz wild mushrooms — an assortment is good,
or you could use just chanterelles;
1 package of halloumi cheese; olive oil; arugula;
freshly ground black pepper; a small handful of fresh
flat-leaf parsley, leaves finely chopped

method Pick over the wild mushrooms, removing any dirt, and wipe clean with a damp cloth (actually washing them gives a soggy texture). Slice the block of cheese across into slices about 1/2in thick — you should have between 6 and 8 slices. Heat the broiler to maximum.

Heat 3 tablespoons of olive oil over medium-high heat. Sauté the wild mushrooms for 5 minutes, until tender. Broil the slices of cheese for 3 to 4 minutes, until tinged with brown. Place on serving plates with a good pile of arugula. Quickly return the mushrooms to high heat to bubble off any liquid, then pile them beside the cheese. Season with pepper, sprinkle with the parsley and serve.

Hot crushed tomato paste

This hot and fiery dip is a favorite among the Kurdish population in the east of Turkey.

1 green bell pepper; 4 medium tomatoes or 2 large beefsteak
tomatoes, about 1lb in total, peeled and seeded;
1/2 large cucumber, peeled;
1 red onion, peeled; sea salt;
1 clove of garlic, peeled and finely chopped;
1 teaspoon dried mint;
1 tablespoon very finely chopped fresh flat-leaf parsley;
1 teaspoon paprika; 1/4 to1/2 teaspoon cayenne pepper;
1 heaped tablespoon red-pepper paste (use tomato paste
mixed with a little more paprika if you can't get this);
1 tablespoon grape or red-wine vinegar;
2 tablespoons extra-virgin olive oil

method Remove the stem and core of the green bell pepper. Now either chop all the vegetables very finely or (much easier) use the food processor. If you take the latter course, be careful not to process them to a mush — you are aiming for a crunchy texture. Put the chopped vegetables in a colander, sprinkle them generously with salt and leave them for 10 minutes or so to drain off the excess juice.

Now mix in the garlic, herbs, seasonings, red-pepper paste, vinegar and oil. Spread on a plate and chill well before serving. If possible, leave until the next day to let the flavors meld and mingle.

pictured on page 35

Stuffed grape leaves

No Greek meze table is complete without dolmades, the dish of stuffed grape leaves that originates from Macedonia and has been adopted throughout Turkey and the Balkans. In winter, the stuffing often includes meat and the grape leaves are served hot as a more substantial course, but I prefer this summer version.

I know you can buy dolmades already made, but they are quite easy, if a little fiddly, to make yourself and really do taste better. And at least you don't need to find fresh grape leaves: in Greek and Turkish markets the leaves are sold cured in brine — just as you will find them in packages in your supermarket.

8oz grape leaves in brine, about 40 leaves;
6 scallions; 2/3 cup olive oil;
21/2 cups light chicken stock;
salt; scant 1 cup long-grain rice;
1 teaspoon ground cinnamon;
6 tablespoons pine nuts;
6 tablespoons raisins; juice of 1 lemon;
3 tablespoons chopped fresh parsley;
2 tablespoons chopped fresh dill;
1 teaspoon dried mint

method Remove the grape leaves from the brine and place in a large bowl. Pour boiling water over the leaves and let stand for 20 minutes.

Finely chop the scallions, including the green part. Heat 2 tablespoons of the oil and fry the scallions for 5 minutes, until soft. Meanwhile, bring the stock to a boil and add salt to taste.

Add the rice and cinnamon to the onions and stir well, making sure the grains of rice become coated in oil. Pour in the boiling stock and leave to simmer for 10 minutes, until all the liquid is absorbed and small holes start to appear in the surface of the rice. Add the pine nuts and raisins, cover with a clean dish towel, followed by the lid, and let stand for 15 minutes.

Meanwhile, drain the grape leaves and then rinse thoroughly under cold running water. Line the base of a large, heavy-bottomed pan with grape leaves. Remove the cover of the rice mixture and stir in half the lemon juice, the fresh chopped herbs and dried mint.

To make each stuffed grape leaf, take a leaf and place it on a surface, stem end toward you. Put a heaped teaspoon of the rice mixture just above the point where the stem joins the leaf. Fold both sides of the leaf into the middle, and then roll the leaf up so you have a cylinder. Put each dolmade, join side down, in the lined pan, packing them tightly against each other.

Pour the remaining oil and lemon juice into the pan and add sufficient water to just cover the dolmades. Place a plate on top and weigh it down with cans. Put the pot over low heat and simmer for 1 hour. Leave the dolmades to cool in the liquid before serving — ideally with fresh lemons and cool, thick yogurt.

pictured on page 45

Zucchini fritters

I owe this recipe to Ismail, who runs the beachside restaurant of the Orange Pansyion in Çirali on Turkey's south-western coastline. Çirali is an extraordinary place. At one end of the wide sweep of bay lies the abandoned site of Olympos; high up in the woods on the mountain at the other end, flame shoots straight out from the rock, the phenomenon known as the *chimera*. And between the two there is a vast expanse of sand, one of the few remaining nesting places for sea turtles. One night my mother and I dined beside this beach, warmed in the cool fall air by a fire of brushwood, eating tidbits such as these little fritters of the local zucchini mixed with cheese and slowly fried while we waited for our freshly grilled fish.

to make 12 fritters   *2 large zucchini, about 11/4lbs*
   in total, preferably the lighter green skinned variety;
coarse sea salt; 1 medium white onion, peeled;
1 fat clove of garlic, peeled;
about 3 tablespoons all-purpose flour;
freshly ground black pepper;
2 tablespoons each of chopped fresh mint,
   dill and flat-leaf parsley; 3 large whole eggs, beaten;
sunflower oil; strained yogurt, to serve

method   Wash the zucchini well then grate coarsely, including the skin. Sprinkle generously with salt (about 1 level teaspoon of the coarse variety) and let stand for 15 minutes or so to weep their juices.

Meanwhile, grate the onion, discarding any juice, and finely chop the clove of garlic. Drain the zucchini and, with your hands, squeeze well to get rid of any extra moisture. Mix together the drained zucchini, onion and garlic.

Sift the flour and season generously with pepper. Add the chopped herbs, the zucchini, onion and garlic mixture, and the beaten eggs. Stir well together with a wooden spoon.

Fill a nonstick skillet with oil to a depth of about 3/4in and place over medium heat. When the oil is hot enough to crisp a cube of bread, start frying the zucchini fritters. Add the mixture a generous tablespoonful at a time to the hot oil, never adding more than 3 or 4 spoonfuls at once or you will overcrowd the pan. With the first patties, stand well back in case the oil spits. Fry for 3 minutes or so, then carefully turn over and fry for 1 to 2 minutes longer. The fritters should be golden brown but still tinged with the green of the zucchini and herbs.

Remove from the oil with a draining spoon and drain on paper towels, then repeat the exercise. This quantity should give you enough for 12 fritters. Serve hot as part of a meze table with spoonfuls of cold yogurt. The fritters are also good cold and can be reheated.

left *Zucchini Fritters* **right** *Stuffed Grape Leaves (p43)*

Salads

In the eastern Mediterranean, salads are served at the start of the meal, rather than after the main course. In Lebanon and Syria, for example, no sooner have you sat down at your restaurant table than a plate of vegetables is placed before you, together with a sharp knife. While you deliberate over what to eat, you are expected to slice open fat, juicy tomatoes and crisp, bright green bell peppers, carve chunks from the heart of a lettuce, munch on vast red radishes, chew sprigs of fresh parsley — all adorned with nothing more than a good pinch of salt. No trendy bowls of olive oil here. But in the Balkans, Turkey and Greece, in good Ottoman style, all the effort is taken away from you. Salads are still ordered as a matter of course at the start of the meal, but someone else has done the chopping. The contents vary according to the season.

Bulgur wheat salad

In Lebanon they have the herb-laden tabbouleh, sharpened with lemon juice; in southeastern Turkey and northern Syria they choose instead to swathe their bulgur wheat salad in a dressing heavy with the essence of tomato and red pepper to make *ksir*. Both versions are best eaten scooped up with crunchy leaves of lettuce.

generous 1/2 cup fine-grain bulgur wheat; 3 large scallions;
2 large beefsteak tomatoes, peeled and seeded;
a large handful of fresh flat-leaf parsley;
a small handful of fresh mint; 1 teaspoon sea salt;
1 romaine lettuce, to serve
for the dressing   *2 tablespoons tomato paste;*
1 tablespoon paprika; 1 teaspoon red pepper flakes;
1 dessertspoon pomegranate syrup (optional);
juice of 1 large lemon; 4 tablespoons extra-virgin olive oil

method   Barely cover the bulgur wheat with boiling water and let stand for 30 minutes. Meanwhile, finely chop the scallions, including the green part. Dice the tomato flesh and finely chop the leaves of the herbs.

To make the dressing, beat together the tomato paste, paprika, red pepper flakes, pomegranate syrup if you have it and lemon juice. Slowly stir in the oil, beating all the time, until you have a well-amalgamated sauce.

Squeeze any remaining moisture from the grains of wheat and then sprinkle in the salt. Stir in the onions, tomatoes and herbs and then add the dressing, stirring well to make sure all the grains are coated.

The salad is best made several hours in advance, to allow the bulgur to take up the other flavors. It should be served at room temperature, not straight from the refrigerator. When you are ready to eat, strip the leaves from the lettuce and wash them. Use the crisp leaves to wrap up bite-size spoonfuls of the salad.

pictured on page 35

Shepherd's salad

A shepherd would take up to the hills in his knapsack a few ripe tomatoes, a bell pepper or two, maybe a fat cucumber and certainly a juicy red onion; and for his lunch he sliced them open with his sharp knife and sprinkled them with salt and fruity olive oil. From this rural fantasy comes the favorite summer salad of the eastern Mediterranean, but of course it has been refined — and with good reason, because the salad tastes so much better when all the ingredients are finely chopped, so their flavors mingle.

2 large beefsteak tomatoes or 4 smaller ones,
*   the riper the better;*
1/2 large or 1 small cucumber, peeled;
2 small or 1 large green bell pepper, stem and seeds removed;
1 red onion, peeled, or 4 small scallions;
2 small fresh green chili peppers (optional);
a good handful of fresh flat-leaf parsley,
*   leaves finely chopped; sea salt; juice of 1 lemon;*
4 to 6 tablespoons extra-virgin olive oil

method Finely dice the tomatoes, cucumber, bell pepper(s) and onion or scallion — the point is that they should be small but distinct. Seed the chili peppers if you are using them and also dice finely. Stir all together and add the parsley. Add a generous seasoning of salt to the lemon juice, then beat in the oil — the exact quantity will depend upon the amount of lemon juice and therefore the size of the lemon, so the answer is to taste to check for balance. Pour the dressing over the salad and (in complete contrast to the usual instructions for salads) let stand for at least 20 minutes before serving.

Preparing a salad at Yassiçal, central Turkey

Winter salad

1/4 medium red cabbage; 2 large carrots, peeled;
2 large, long white radishes, peeled;
a bag of arugula, preferably the smaller-leaved wild variety;
juice of 1 large lemon; 6 tablespoons extra-virgin olive oil;
sea salt and freshly ground black pepper;
a few fronds of fresh dill

method Remove the tough outer leaves and the core from the cabbage, then grate it finely. Also grate the carrots and radishes — once again, finely.

On a serving plate, make 3 piles of the grated vegetables, leaving a fourth quarter for the arugula. Whisk together the lemon juice and olive oil, season well and pour over the vegetables. Scatter with the dill and serve.

Beet salad

This is a Lebanese recipe, given a distinctive flavor by the pomegranate molasses.

8 small fresh uncooked beets in their skins;
1/2 large or 1 small white onion, peeled and finely chopped;
a large handful of fresh flat-leaf parsley, finely chopped;
a small handful of fresh mint, finely chopped;
1 fat clove of garlic, peeled and minced;
1 teaspoon sea salt; juice of 1 large lemon;
1 tablespoon pomegranate molasses;
4 tablespoons extra-virgin olive oil

method Steam the beets for about 45 minutes, until they are tender. As soon as they are cool enough to handle, peel off and discard the skins. Dice the flesh and mix with the chopped onion, herbs and garlic. Whisk the salt into the lemon, followed by the molasses. Slowly whisk in the oil, until you have a thick emulsion. Pour this over the beets (it's important to do this while the beets are hot, so the flavors are absorbed) and let stand for several hours before serving.

variation You can also simply dress the beets with a mixture of 1 cup of strained yogurt and 2 tablespoons extra-virgin olive oil. In this case, you might like to purée the salad, rather than leaving the beets in dice, and serve it as a dip.

Eggplant salad

The eggplant was always the king of Ottoman vegetables; so it is perhaps little wonder that today in Syria and the Lebanon this dish of garlicky eggplant purée is known as poor man's caviar.

5 medium eggplants,
  about 2 1/2 lbs in total;
3 cloves of garlic, peeled and finely chopped;
sea salt; juice of 1 large lemon;
4 to 6 tablespoons extra-virgin olive oil

method Heat the broiler to maximum. Prick each eggplant several times with a skewer (this prevents them exploding while under the broiler) and place under the heat. Broil for 20 minutes, turning several times, until the skin is black and blistered all over.

As soon as the eggplants are cool enough to handle, peel off the skins and then squeeze as much moisture as you can from the flesh. Place the flesh on a wooden board and mash with a fork, adding the garlic. Scrape into a bowl and add a generous seasoning of salt and the lemon juice. Slowly add the olive oil, stirring all the time, until the eggplant acquires an unctuous quality; the exact amount of oil needed will depend upon the eggplants. Spread the salad over a flat plate and let stand (but not in the refrigerator) for several hours before serving, to let the flavors meld. Traditionally, the salad is garnished with a few black olives.

pictured on page 35

Cheese mixed with tomato and onion

Shanklish is a particular kind of cheese that has given its name to a classic Lebanese meze dish. Made from cow's milk, it is salted, fermented and flavored with thyme and pepper. I enjoyed it at its finest in the high Bekaa Valley, where they have been making wine for some three thousand years, and M. Hochar of Château Musar still carries on the privilege. The children of the Bekaa, he told me, eat the *shanklish* with cucumber, tomato and bread at school. Meanwhile, in the restaurants of Beirut, it is made into a salad, mixed with *za'atar* (a wild thyme), sumac, tomatoes and onions. *Shanklish* is difficult to get outside its area (unless you have a local Lebanese merchant), but a good salad, if not quite the same thing, can be made using feta cheese.

7oz feta cheese; several sprigs of fresh thyme,
  leaves stripped; freshly ground black pepper;
2 teaspoons sumac; juice of 1/2 lemon;
4 tablespoons extra-virgin olive oil;
2 large tomatoes, peeled, seeded and finely diced;
1 red onion, peeled and diced;
a large handful of fresh flat-leaf parsley, finely chopped

method Using your fingers, break up the feta. Sprinkle over the leaves of thyme, a generous seasoning of pepper and the sumac. Beat together the lemon juice and oil and pour this over the cheese. Let stand for several hours.

When you want to eat the salad, stir the tomato, onion and parsley into the cheese and eat with lots of bread.

Salads with yogurt
Whenever you are served a vegetable dish in Turkey, you can expect to find a creamy mound of yogurt on the side of the plate, and it is also a popular accompaniment to various grilled or broiled meats. But in some salads, the yogurt becomes the very point of the dish.

Fava bean purée

2lbs young fava beans in their pods;
4 or 5 scallions; 2 fat cloves of garlic, peeled;
1/2 cup olive oil; sea salt and
*   freshly ground black pepper; 4 tablespoons water;*
2 tablespoons finely chopped fresh dill fronds;
juice of 1/2 lemon; 2 tablespoons strained yogurt,
*   preferably made from sheep's milk*

method   Pod the beans and blanch them in boiling water for 30 seconds. Now slip off the tough white, outer skins.

Finely chop the scallions, including the green parts, and the garlic. Heat 2 tablespoons of the olive oil in a heavy pan over medium heat and add the garlic and scallions. Cook for 3 to 4 minutes, until the onions are soft. Now add the beans and cook, stirring all the time, for another 2 minutes. Add the seasoning, measured water and dill (reserving a few sprigs) and leave to cook for 5 minutes, until the beans are soft and the liquid has evaporated.

Purée the mixture in a food processor. Slowly add the lemon juice, the yogurt and remaining olive oil, so you have a smooth, creamy, light green paste. Scatter with the remaining fronds of dill and serve with bread.

Cucumber and yogurt salad

Known as *tsatsiki* in Greece and *caçik* in Turkey (and also very popular in Egypt, Lebanon and Syria), this is the most refreshing of salads in summer.

2 medium cucumbers, about 1lb in total;
1 teaspoon sea salt; a good pinch of white sugar;
2 cloves of garlic, peeled and finely chopped;
1 teaspoon dried mint; 13/4 cups strained yogurt;
2 tablespoons iced water

method   First peel the cucumbers. Cut them in half lengthwise, and cut each half into 4 again lengthwise, then cut across at regular intervals so you end up with small cubes. Sprinkle the cucumber flesh with the salt and sugar and let stand for 10 minutes.

Pour off the excess water given out by the cucumber and, with your hands, squeeze any more moisture from the flesh. Beat the garlic and mint into the yogurt together with the 2 tablespoons of iced water, then stir in the cucumber dice. Chill very well before serving.

note   In summer, this mixture is often diluted with iced water and served as soup, with ice cubes floating in it (see page 26).

Yogurt with garlic and watercress

Stopping at a trout restaurant in the wooded hills above Turkey's southern coast, we found our table beside a natural spring that fed into the trout stream. In the cool waters bunches of watercress and hearts of romaine lettuce floated; whenever a waiter wanted salad, he simply picked out a bunch and shook the drops free. Served as a precursor to the barbecued trout, this mixture of garlicky yogurt and peppery green leaves was the perfect cooling appetizer.

1 cup thick, strained yogurt;
2 fat cloves of garlic, peeled and minced;
sea salt and freshly ground black pepper;
1 bunch of watercress, rinsed and drained;
2 tablespoons extra-virgin olive oil

method Mix the garlic into the yogurt and then add plenty of seasoning. Arrange the watercress on a plate, spoon over the garlicky yogurt, dribble over the oil and chill well before serving.

variation In season, you can substitute purslane for the watercress. Distinguished by its fleshy stems and green, slightly furred leaves, it has a subtler flavor.

Eggplants with yogurt

2 eggplants, 8-10oz each; olive oil;
2 cloves of garlic, peeled; 1/2 teaspoon coarse sea salt;
a good handful of fresh mint leaves;
11/4 cups strained yogurt, preferably sheep's milk

method Heat the oven to 400°F. Place the whole, washed eggplants in the oven and bake for 20 minutes. Now split the eggplants lengthwise, leaving them still attached at the stem, and carefully pry them open. Brush the cut surface with olive oil and return to the oven for another 40 minutes, until the surface is brown and the flesh tender.

Meanwhile, crush the peeled garlic cloves with the salt in a mortar and pestle. Add the mint leaves and crush again. Stir in the strained yogurt.

With a sharp knife, score the cut surface of the cooked eggplant several times lengthwise. Press the flesh down and pile the yogurt mixture on top. Serve straight away, with a spoon so you can scoop out the warm, tender eggplant flesh and the cool, minty yogurt.

Sheep grazing on Crete — sheep's milk yogurt is especially rich and creamy

above *preparing* böreği, *Turkey* **opposite** *Cheese "Cigars" (p54)*

Pastries

The original Turks were nomads from the grasslands bordering China and Mongolia, and it is from this heritage that their delectable pastries are believed to originate, as descendants of the dumplings still favored in Mongolian and Chinese kitchens. The most traditional *böreği* are made with watered pastry filled with cheese, but there is a wide variety of pastries and fillings — and *böreği* can be fried, baked, steamed or boiled. Whatever variety you choose, no meze table can be complete without a plateful of *böreği*.

Pastries similar to the Turkish *böreği* are found all around the eastern Mediterranean. Some of my favorites include the little *spanakopittes* from Greece, phyllo pastry filled with feta cheese and the wild greens known as *horta*; the Lebanese *sambousik*, piecrust pastry with a spicy lamb, pine nut and raisin filling; and *pasteles*, little pies made of olive oil pastry with an eggplant filling.

a note on pastry   In Turkey, a delicate pastry known as *yufka* is made; *yufka* comes in different shapes and sizes, from the vast rounds used for *gözleme* (see page 114) to the much finer, paper-thin version that wraps up the famous "cigar" pastries. Even Turkish housewives buy their *yufka*, because making it is a great art. If you do not have a Turkish store near you, use phyllo pastry dough.

Cheese "cigars"

These pastries owe their name to their torpedo shape.

makes 8 to 12 pastries   *6oz feta cheese, drained;*
1 extra-large egg; 1 tablespoon finely chopped fresh dill;
1 tablespoon finely chopped fresh mint;
2 tablespoons finely chopped fresh flat-leaf parsley;
freshly ground black pepper; 1 package of yufka
   or phyllo pastry (minimum 12 sheets);
sunflower oil for deep-frying

method   Crumble the feta and mash together with the egg and the chopped herbs. Add pepper to taste.

Take a sheet of pastry dough about 31/4in wide (depending on the shape of the dough you have bought, you might have to cut the pastry into 1 or 2 long strips). Keep the rest of the dough covered with a damp dish towel.

to assemble the pastries   Place a generous teaspoon of the cheese mixture at the end closest to you. Carefully fold in a 1/2in border the length of the strip then roll it up to make a cigar shape. Moisten the end with water, place the "cigar" on a plate and cover with another damp dish towel.

to cook the pastries   Fill a skillet with oil deep enough to cover the pastries. Heat the oil and, when it is hot enough to turn a cube of bread golden, add the pastries a few at a time. They are cooked when they turn golden brown. Drain on paper towels and serve piping hot.

pictured on page 53

Pastries with pastirma and cheese

Pastirma is meat that has been preserved with spices, red pepper and garlic. It originates from the need to cure meat after slaughter and was once made with goat and camel meat as well as the more typical beef or veal. To put it into pastries was a sign of wanton indulgence, typical of the palace kitchens. It pleases me, therefore, that I originally tasted this rich snack in the magnificent former soup kitchen beside the ornate tombs of Sultan Suleyman the Magnificent's family in the first Ottoman capital of Bursa. I later discovered that it has become popular throughout Turkey, and I prefer the southern version cooked with olive oil rather than dripping in butter. And it may not be very Ottoman, but processed cheese really does do the job.

for 6 pastries   *6 slices of phyllo dough; 12 slices of* pastirma,
   any rind removed; 6 thin slices of processed cooking cheese;
7oz feta cheese; chopped fresh dill;
extra-virgin olive oil

method   Heat the oven to 400°F. Lay out a sheet of phyllo dough, keeping the remainder covered with a damp cloth. Lay the *pastirma* on it then carefully roll over to cover. Add a slice of the processed cheese and roll again. Sprinkle the surface with a little of the feta and dill and roll again. The aim is to have a flat, thin pastry with 3 layers of filling. Repeat for the other pastries.

Keep the pastries covered with a damp cloth until you are ready to cook them. Dribble generously with olive oil and cook in the heated oven until brown and crisp. Serve piping hot and eat with your fingers.

Spinach and cheese pastries

In Greece these are made with whatever greens can be picked from the hillside or the vegetable garden — popular choices include Swiss or red chard and the tops of beets. Spinach makes a practical alternative. If the making of individual bundles seems too complicated (although it is a lot easier than it sounds), you can also make one large round pie with overlapping layers of phyllo.

22oz fresh spinach; 2 tablespoons olive oil;
4 scallions, finely chopped, including green parts;
a good pinch of grated nutmeg;
sea salt and freshly ground black pepper;
1/2 cup ricotta cheese;
4oz feta cheese, drained;
a good handful of fresh flat-leaf parsley,
   leaves finely chopped; 4 tablespoons unsalted butter;
1 package of phyllo pastry dough

method   Wash the spinach very thoroughly, then drain, leaving some drops of water clinging to the leaves. Pack into a heavy-bottomed pan and place over medium heat. Cover and let cook down for 5 minutes or so, stirring once or twice to prevent sticking to the bottom. When the spinach completely breaks down, drain and immediately refresh with cold running water. With your hands, squeeze out excess water. Chop the spinach finely.

Heat the oil in a heavy skillet and add the scallions. Cook for 5 minutes or so, until the onions are tender. Add the chopped spinach, the nutmeg, plenty of pepper and a little salt (the feta is salty). Stir well, cook for a 1 minute longer, take off the heat and let cool.

With a fork, mash the two cheeses together, seasoning with a little more pepper, but not any salt. When the spinach mixture is completely cool, add the cheese and parsley and stir all well together with a fork.

When you are ready to cook the pastries, heat the oven to 350°F. Melt the butter and skim off any scum.

Open your package of phyllo pastry dough, making sure the sheets are kept covered with a damp cloth.

to assemble the pastries   Traditionally these pastries are made in a triangular shape. Take a rectangular sheet of the dough and cut it in half lengthwise. Brush a little melted butter along the length of the strip then pile a heaped teaspoon of the filling in the bottom right-hand corner (or the other side if you are left-handed). Fold the left-hand corner over the filling to form a triangle at the bottom of the strip, then fold the right-hand corner through 180 degrees so the triangle moves up the sheet of phyllo. Pick up the new right-hand corner and fold it over to the left-hand side, then fold the left-hand corner through 180 degrees. Continue the process until you reach the end of the phyllo — and, believe me, it is simpler than it sounds.

When you have your triangle, brush the surface of the dough with melted butter, and place on a baking tray with the seam underneath. Carry on making pastries until you run out of either filling or dough.

to cook the pastries   Bake the pastries in the heated oven for 15 to 20 minutes, until crisp and golden. They are at their best served warm.

Little pies with eggplant

These *pasteles* are believed to have originated among the Spanish-speaking Jewish community that migrated to Ottoman lands after the collapse of the Moorish Empire. Today they are particular favorites in Istanbul and Izmir.

for the filling *1 large eggplant, about 10oz; sea salt; 4 tablespoons olive oil; 1 medium onion, peeled and finely chopped; 1 teaspoon sugar; 1 teaspoon ground cumin; freshly ground black pepper; 2 medium tomatoes, peeled, seeded and diced;*
for the pastry *2 cups all-purpose flour; 1/2 teaspoon sea salt; 4 tablespoons olive oil; 3 to 4 tablespoons warm water; 1 egg yolk; sesame seeds*

Café Naufara, Damascus, Syria

method Dice the eggplant, sprinkle generously with salt, place in a colander with a plate on top to weigh the eggplant down and let drain for 30 minutes.

Heat the oil for the filling and fry the onion for 10 minutes, until golden. Rinse the eggplant well and pat dry with a cloth then add the eggplant to the pan, together with the sugar, cumin and a generous grind of pepper. Cook over low heat, stirring regularly to prevent the eggplant from sticking, for 15 minutes or so, until tender. Now add the tomatoes and continue to cook over a low heat for another 15 minutes, again stirring from time to time. Turn the heat up for the last minute of cooking and drain off any excess oil the eggplant releases. Mash the mixture up with a fork and leave to cool.

Meanwhile, turn your attention to the pastry dough, which happily is very simple to make and does not need any resting. Sift the flour with the salt and then, with a wooden spoon, stir in the oil. Slowly add the warm water, stirring all the time, until the pastry starts to stick together — you might need a little more or a little less, depending upon the flour. Give the dough a quick knead for 30 seconds or so, until you have a smooth ball, and there you have it.

Heat the oven to 400°F. Divide the pastry in half and roll one half out on a floured work surface. With a cookie cutter (in fact, I use a cup), cut out 6 circles, each approximately 31/2 inches in diameter. Place a teaspoon of the filling in the middle of each and fold over to form a half-moon shape. Crimp the edges together with your fingers and place on a greased baking tray. Repeat the process with the remaining dough so you end up with 12 little pies.

Brush the surface of the pastries with the egg yolk and sprinkle with the sesame seeds. Place in the heated oven and bake for 30 minutes, until lightly golden. The pastries are at their best served warm from the oven.

Lebanese meat pastries

for the pastry   *12/3 cups all-purpose flour;
a good pinch of salt; 4 tablespoons unsalted butter;
1 tablespoon olive oil; 4 to 6 tablespoons cold water;
beaten egg yolk, for glazing*

method   Sift the flour and salt together and make a few
holes in the surface of the flour. Melt the butter and oil
together, taking care not to let it brown. Leave to cool
slightly then pour the melted fat into the holes in the flour.
Quickly add 4 tablespoons cold water and work together
with your hands. If necessary, add a little more cold water,
until you have a dough. Handle as little as possible and
refrigerate for 30 minutes.

for the filling   *2 tablespoons butter; 1 tablespoon olive oil;
1 heaped tablespoon pine nuts;
1 small onion, peeled and finely chopped;
6oz ground lamb;
salt and freshly ground black pepper;
1/2 teaspoon ground cinnamon; 1/2 teaspoon allspice;
1 heaped tablespoon chopped fresh flat-leaf parsley;
4 teaspoons sumac (optional)*

method   To make the filling, heat the butter and oil in a
heavy-bottomed skillet over medium heat and toast the
pine nuts until golden brown (be careful — they burn
easily). Remove the nuts with a draining spoon and drain
on paper towels. Add the chopped onion to the oil and
butter in the pan and fry for 5 minutes, stirring regularly,
until golden brown. Now add the ground meat, together
with plenty of seasoning and the cinnamon and allspice.
Cook for 4 to 5 minutes longer, stirring all the time, until the
meat is brown. Take off the heat and stir in the chopped
parsley and pine nuts (and sumac, if used). Let cool.

to assemble the pastries   Roll out the dough thinly and cut
out about 12 x 31/4- to 31/2-in circles. Place a little of the
meat mixture in the middle of each and then fold the circle
over. Crimp the edge of each pastry with the back of a fork
to both seal and give a crinkled effect.

to cook the pastries   Heat the oven to 400°F. Brush the
surface of the pastries with melted butter and place on a
greased baking tray. Bake for 15 minutes then brush the
surface with the beaten egg yolk. Bake for 10 minutes
longer until golden brown. Serve warm.

Playing dominoes, Tripoli, Lebanon

Bottarga with garlic and oil

Just as Londoners once protested against the excess of oysters, so the people of Constantinople exclaimed their boredom with caviar from the Black Sea. But these days the sturgeon is an endangered fish (even in Turkey it is now usually sourced from Iran) and a new kind of caviar has acquired fans — the pressed roe of the gray mullet.

At its very best, it comes in a sausage shape encased with yellow wax, as it is sold in Istanbul's Egyptian spice bazaar. In Pandeli's, the famous Greek-owned restaurant that sits above the entrance to the bazaar, you can sit surrounded by blue faience tiles gazing out at the Golden Horn and enjoying this exquisite delicacy. But there they serve it perfectly plain whereas in Lebanon, as usual, they take it one step farther, adding thin slivers of raw garlic and a dribble of the finest olive oil to offset the strong taste of the roe (below).

Bottarga should be well chilled before eating and served with the yellow wax intact for it to keep its shape as you slice it finely across. Of course you should not eat this wax, as I have seen a few unfortunate diners do, but peel the fine outer coating off with your fingers.

Süleymaniye Mosque from Galata Bridge, Istanbul, Turkey

Mussels in beer batter

Along the shores of the Bosphorus, and especially around Istanbul's Galata Bridge, from where the commuter ferries set off, these little mussels, deep-fried in crisp batter, are a favorite snack. In Ottoman times the batter would have been made with fresh yeast for lightness, but beer provides a practical and rapid alternative.

3lbs mussels in their shells;
3/4 cups all-purpose flour;
1 teaspoon salt; 2 extra-large eggs; 1 cup beer;
sunflower oil for deep-frying; 1 lemon, quartered, to serve

method Wash and scrub the mussels and remove the beards. Place them in a pot, covered with a lid, over high heat and briefly steam them open in their own liquid — 2 to 3 minutes should be enough. Let cool.

Sift the flour with the salt. Separate the eggs and beat the yolks. Make a well in the middle of the flour and add the yolks. Now very slowly pour in the beer, stirring all the time with a wooden spoon. Your aim should be to bring in all the flour from the edges of the bowl. Continue stirring until you have added all the beer and you have a smooth batter. Let stand for half an hour or so.

Meanwhile, pick the mussels out of their shells, discarding any whose shells are cracked or have not opened.

When you are ready to cook the mussels (and, perhaps more importantly, eat them — they must be eaten right away), fill a skillet to a depth of 3/4 inch with the oil and place over medium heat. Whisk the egg whites until stiff and fold gently into the batter. When the oil is hot enough to crisp a cube of bread, dip a few mussels at a time in the batter and transfer to the hot oil: never overcrowd the pan. Cook the mussels for a minute or two, until the batter turns golden, and remove with a draining spoon; drain on paper towels. Serve very hot with the wedges of lemon to squeeze over. Traditionally these mussels are served with *tarator* sauce (see Fish Kabobs, page 72).

variations Deep-fried rings of calamari or squid are also often served with *tarator* sauce. A simple sauce of chopped fresh garlic, fresh lemon and extra-virgin olive oil is a delicious alternative.

on the barbecue

Kabobs were the ideal food for an army on the move, although more often than not the Ottoman army, priding itself on its speed of movement, had to make do with rice and whatever greens and berries they could gather. But when they had the chance to erect their ornate tents (and reputedly they could set up the equivalent of a small town in less than two hours), they would gather firewood, slaughter sheep or goats, and either grill the meat over charcoal or build a fire over which to stew *firin* kabobs — one-pot meals cooked in the cauldrons that for the janissaries were the equivalent of their regimental colors. And on victory days they would have time to dig a pit, fill it with wood and cook a whole lamb.

Of course, grilling meat over wood was not a new idea — it is one of the oldest cooking methods in the world, and certainly one used by the original Turkic peoples when they were still roaming the steppes. But what was unusual for the time was that the court cooks of Topkapi Palace recognized the unique flavor given to meat and fish when cooked over fragrant wood and elevated this method of expedience to one of refined elegance.

The Ottomans were confirmed barbecuers. And the habit has not been lost in modern Turkey. Grilled meat is still the favorite food for high days and holidays, and consumers expect to see the food cooked before their eyes. There are plenty of restaurants where (in good steppes style) a barbecue is brought to each individual table, with simply a pile of meat and a plate of raw vegetables, so diners can cook to their individual satisfaction. Then, of course, there is the doner kabob, actually a fairly recent invention, claimed from the nineteenth century by Iskender's restaurant in Bursa. But that is not something you will want to prepare at home.

Kabobs

The Turks like to claim that, like much else besides, the habit of grilling chunks of meat over charcoal originated in the Caucasus, from where it spread across the Mediterranean. Who knows, but certainly the Turks are masters of the kabob. For the classic *şiş kebabi*, streetsellers pride themselves on the quality of their marinade, be it yogurt and spices or olive oil, lemon juice and fresh herbs.

for the kabobs   *boned shoulder or leg of lamb, cut into generous cubes; about 11/2lbs should feed 4 of normal appetite, although it would certainly be insufficient for a Turk*

2 alternative marinades   *1 large white onion, peeled and chopped into fine half rings; juice of 2 lemons; 6 tablespoons extra-virgin olive oil; sea salt and freshly ground black pepper; a good handful of fresh flat-leaf parsley; a few sprigs of fresh thyme*

or

1 cup thick strained yogurt; 1 teaspoon freshly ground black pepper; 1/2 teaspoon sea salt; 1 teaspoon paprika; 1/2 teaspoon cayenne pepper (or to taste); 1 tablespoon tomato paste

method   Whichever you choose, mix together all the marinade ingredients and pour over the meat. Leave, overnight if possible, stirring the meat once or twice to make sure it is evenly coated. When you want to cook the meat, get the barbecue coals glowing (or, if you must, heat the broiler to maximum). Shake the meat free of the marinade and thread onto skewers, a few pieces on each. Cook until nicely charred on the outside but still pink on the inside — cut into a piece to see. Ideally, serve with lots of flat bread and a salad or two.

Adana kabob

Kabobs are made from ground lamb as well as whole chunks of meat. This spicy version comes from Adana in the southeast of Turkey. It is traditionally served on a sword, but a flat-bladed skewer will do well.

11/2lbs lamb, finely ground;
4 small dried red chili peppers (or more if you like it hot);
1 teaspoon sea salt;
1 teaspoon freshly ground black pepper;
2 small red onions, peeled and finely chopped;
3 cloves of garlic, peeled and minced;
2 large handfuls of fresh flat-leaf parsley;
8 long, flat skewers; 2 lemons, quartered, to serve

method   Add the seasonings to the lamb, followed by the onions, garlic and parsley. In the food processor, give the meat a quick whizz — the texture should be fine and the contents well mixed. Otherwise you will need to knead it well with your hands. Leave the meat to stand for several hours to absorb the flavors.

When you are ready to cook, either get the barbecue coals going (the best choice) or heat the broiler to maximum. Dampen your hands with warm water and pull off a piece of the meat mixture about the size of an egg. With your hands, mold this down the skewer, making a flat sausage shape and leaving a gap at each end. Cook over or under the heat for 4 to 5 minutes on each side, until cooked through. Serve with lemon to squeeze over the kabobs and lots of bread; grilled green bell peppers with yogurt are a good accompaniment.

previous pages barbecuing sardines on the Bosphorus **opposite** *Adana Kabob*

Lamb kabobs with yogurt

Meat kabobs served on flat bread with fresh tomato sauce and thick creamy yogurt make a complete meal. This mildly spiced version is based on a dish I enjoyed in Damascus.

for the kabobs   *1 1/2lbs lamb, shoulder or leg,*
  trimmed into bite-size pieces;
1 large mild onion, peeled and grated;
juice of 1 lemon; 2 tablespoons olive oil;
2 fat cloves of garlic, peeled and crushed;
1 teaspoon ground cumin; 1 teaspoon paprika;
a sprig of fresh thyme; sea salt and freshly ground black pepper
for the sauce   *3 tablespoons olive oil;*
24oz tomatoes, peeled, seeded and chopped;
a good pinch of sugar; 1 teaspoon tomato paste;
salt and freshly ground black pepper
to serve   *2 pita or other flat bread;*
1 1/2 cups thick strained yogurt, at room temperature;
2 tablespoons pine nuts; 1 teaspoon paprika;
a good handful of flat-leaf parsley, leaves roughly chopped

method   Mix together all the kabob ingredients. Marinade for at least 3 to 4 hours, turning the meat once or twice.

For the tomato sauce, heat 1 tablespoon of the olive oil in a pan and add the chopped tomato with the sugar, tomato paste and some seasoning. Sweat slowly for 10 minutes, stirring regularly.

Remove the meat from the marinade and thread onto skewers. Grill or broil, preferably over charcoal, for 4 to 5 minutes on either side, basting with the marinade.

While the meat is cooking, split the breads in half length-wise and toast until lightly brown on both sides. Break into squares and scatter over the bottom of the serving dish. Spread the tomato sauce over the bread. Lay the kabobs on top of the tomato and bread and cover with the yogurt.

Briefly toast the pine nuts until golden. Warm the remaining oil and stir in the paprika. Pour the oil over the yogurt and scatter with the pine nuts and parsley.

Lamb and eggplant kabob

2 medium eggplants, 7 to 8oz each;
sea salt; 1 1/4lbs ground lamb;
2 teaspoons paprika; 1 teaspoon red pepper flakes;
1 teaspoon sumac (optional);
1/2 teaspoon freshly ground black pepper; olive oil;
4 metal skewers

method   Cut off the tops and bottoms of the eggplants then cut each across at intervals of roughly 3/4 inch — you should end up with 6 slices per eggplant. Sprinkle generously with salt and leave in a colander for half an hour to drain.

Meanwhile, add the spices to the meat, together with a little salt, and pound the meat well to a smooth texture. Form into 8 separate balls of roughly equal size.

Rinse the eggplants and pat dry. Place a ball of meat on top of a slice of eggplant and flatten it out to fit the shape. Place another slice of eggplant on top of the meat, followed by another ball of meat and then a final slice of eggplant. Push a skewer through the lot and lay on its side on a greased baking tray. Repeat the process so you end up with 4 kabobs. Brush the surface of the eggplant liberally with oil.

By this stage you should either have the barbecue coals glowing or the broiler heated to maximum. Cook the kabobs, turning regularly and basting with oil, for 20 to 25 minutes, until the surface of the eggplants is darkened and crinkly and the meat nicely browned.

Lamb with eggplant purée

Hünkâr beğendi, the Turkish name of this dish, translates as "the queen was pleased" — the queen in question being Empress Eugénie, wife of Napoleon III, who enjoyed the hospitality of the Sultan on a visit to Istanbul in 1862. According to historian Jason Goodwin, the Empress was so impressed with this dish she sent her own chef down to the palace's kitchens to get the recipe. This infuriated the Sultan's chef, who threw out his visitor with the words "an imperial chef cooks with his feelings, his eyes and his nose." Well, quite, but a recipe helps, too.

4 small or 3 large eggplants, 11/2-13/4lbs in total;
6 tablespoons unsalted butter;
1 large Spanish onion, peeled and finely chopped;
salt and freshly ground black pepper;
1lb diced boneless lamb, either shoulder or leg;
4 tomatoes, about 13oz in total, peeled, seeded and
  chopped; 2 tablespoons tomato paste;
21/4 cups water; 1 teaspoon white sugar;
juice of 1/2 lemon; 2 level tablespoons all-purpose flour;
11/4 cups whole milk; 1/2 cup grated hard cheese
  (if you can't get Turkish cheese, use Gruyère)

method Prick each eggplant several times with a fork. Place on a glowing barbecue or, failing that, under a hot broiler. Cook for 20 to 25 minutes, depending on size, turning regularly, until the skin is thoroughly black and the flesh feels soft to the touch.

Meanwhile, melt half the butter in a large, heavy skillet and add the chopped onion. Cook over medium heat, stirring regularly, until tender and lightly golden — about 10 minutes. Season the meat well and add to the pan, continuing to fry for about 5 minutes, until lightly brown all over. Now add the chopped tomatoes, tomato paste, water and sugar. Stir all well together, bring to a boil, turn down to a gentle simmer and let cook, uncovered, for 50 minutes or so, until the meat is tender and the sauce thick. Don't forget to stir occasionally and add a little more water if the sauce is becoming too dry.

While the meat is cooking, turn your attention back to the eggplants. When they are nicely black, take them off the barbecue or out from under the broiler. As soon as they are cool enough to handle, peel off the skin. With a fork, mash the flesh with the lemon juice; set aside.

Melt the remaining butter in a heavy-bottomed pan and stir in the flour. Cook for 30 seconds or so, stirring all the time, until the mixture is golden. Slowly stir in the milk, making sure there are no lumps. Continue to stir while the sauce comes to a boil, and allow to bubble for a minute or so, then take off the heat and stir in the grated cheese, followed by the mashed eggplant. Again mash well together with a fork, until you have a reasonably smooth mixture, then let stand for 10 minutes or so.

to serve arrange the eggplant purée on a plate and make a hole in the middle. Spoon on the meat, together with the tomato and onion sauce.

Marinated grilled quails

*8 quail; 7oz strained yogurt (preferably made
from sheep's milk); 2 tablespoons olive oil;
2 teaspoons tomato paste; 1 teaspoon sweet paprika;
1/2 teaspoon cayenne; salt and freshly ground black pepper;
4 large metal skewers*

method Beat together the yogurt and olive oil. Add the
tomato paste, spices and seasoning and stir well. Dip the
quail in this mixture until they are thoroughly covered,
making sure some of the yogurt mixture goes inside the
cavity. Cover and let marinate for at least 6 hours,
preferably overnight.

The quails are best cooked over charcoal, but they can
also be cooked under a broiler, heated to maximum. If
using a conventional broiler, make sure you place a metal
tray underneath to catch the juices.

Shake off any excess marinade and thread 2 quail onto
each skewer, piercing them at an angle from wing to leg.
Cook, turning regularly, until the outside is golden brown
and no blood runs when you pull the leg away from the
breast: This will take between 20 and 25 minutes under the
broiler, less over charcoal.

Marinated chicken wings

The Lebanese vie with the Turks for mastery of the barbecue,
but they are certainly the masters of this simple dish of
marinated chicken wings. Charred from the heat, they are
often eaten as part of a meze, but also make a dish in their
own right. Serve them with a classic Lebanese salad of wild
arugula mixed with leaves of fresh thyme and dressed with
sea salt and fruity olive oil.

*2lbs chicken wings; juice and grated zest of 2 lemons,
preferably from unwaxed fruit;
1 teaspoon sea salt; freshly ground black pepper;
1 large white onion, peeled and finely chopped;
3 or 4 fat cloves of garlic, peeled and finely chopped;
8 or so sprigs of fresh thyme (lemon thyme if you can get it);
4 tablespoons extra-virgin olive oil*

method Arrange the chicken wings in a large tray,
preferably earthenware, in which they will all lie flat.
Sprinkle the lemon juice and zest over, and add the salt and
a generous seasoning of pepper, the onion and the garlic
and the leaves stripped from the thyme. Finally, pour the oil
over. Let marinate for at least 4 hours, preferably overnight,
turning halfway through.

Either cook the wings over charcoal or under a very hot
broiler. You will need to turn them several times and baste
them with the marinade. They should be lightly charred,
even black in places: 20 to 25 minutes of cooking.

above *half-timbered Ottoman houses border the river in Amasya, central Anatolia* **right** *bedouin women making bread, Syria*

The Ottoman house — and kitchen Within their large

wooden houses, bedecked with graceful balconies and surrounded with

windows, the Ottomans were the masters of studio living. Cohabiting in

extended family groups, the spacious rooms were designed for a multitude of

purposes. Typically, each light and airy space was ringed on three sides with

divans covered in cushions, which at night could be pulled down onto the floor

to sleep on. The bedding was concealed in a cupboard, which in more

sophisticated houses also doubled as the toilet. When it was time to eat, a low

table was put in the middle of the room, around which the diners gathered to select from communal dishes. Because houses might contain up to four generations, not everyone always ate together — and usually the men ate first. One room was normally devoted to cooking, where the women turned out meals for the entire extended family.

Nights could be cold, especially on the Anatolian plain, so each room had a central stove. Cooking was done over an open fire as well as on the stovetop. Not surprisingly, given the typical wooden construction, fire was a frequent problem — one reason why in Istanbul so few of these houses still stand. Today, those that remain are rapidly being converted into stylish city hotels, but venture out into central Anatolia, to towns like Safranbolu and Amasya, and you will still find families living (and eating) in traditional style. And the style of building spread. In Aleppo, Syria, the Armenians of the Ottoman Empire built a whole enclave of such houses, many of which are now under restoration, while Budapest also boasts many of these gracious wooden structures.

But houses (and particularly the kitchen) were for winter. In summer, much of the cooking took place in the courtyard and tasks from pickling and preserving to charcoal-grilling of kabobs were undertaken outside. To alleviate the more tedious tasks, the women of the village or neighborhood gathered in groups, so they could gossip while they worked.

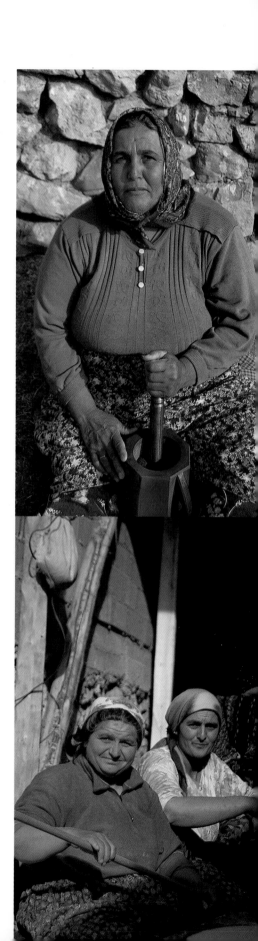

opposite *top: pounding nigella seeds, Yassiçal, central Turkey; bottom: making bread, central Turkey* **above** *Ottoman houses at El Mali, Turkey*

Travel through the countryside today and you will still see women boiling

up *pekmez* (a concentrated grape syrup) over open fires, pounding

nigella and sesame seeds for bread with a mortar and pestle or rolling out

the thin, flat bread that is such a staple.

Fish kabobs

One of the early characteristics of the cooks of the Ottoman Empire was their fondness for nuts used in savory dishes. In this they were not alone in the medieval world — one of the culinary signatures of the Moorish invaders of Spain was a combination of fruits and nuts with meat. But while in al-Andaluz the pine nut and the almond were the most popular nuts, in colder Constantinople the more northerly walnut and hazelnuts were the favorites. This sauce of walnuts crushed with garlic, bread, lemon juice and plenty of olive oil is believed to have a long history.

    Tarator sauce can be served with chicken, but it is most commonly found alongside barbecued fish, particularly fish kabobs. *Tarator* sauce is also very popular with fish in Lebanon, Syria and Egypt, where it is usually made with pine nuts rather than walnuts. However, confusingly, the name *taratoor* is also often given in these countries to a sauce of sesame seed paste flavored with plenty of lemon juice and garlic, which is again served with fish.

Fish market by Galata Bridge, Istanbul, Turkey

for the kabobs   *1lb firm white fish — swordfish would be typical — cut into slices at least 1 inch thick; juice of 1 lemon; 4 tablespoons olive oil; 1 teaspoon sweet paprika; salt and pepper; 16 fresh bay leaves; kabob sticks; 1 lemon, quartered, to serve*

for the sauce   *2 cups shelled, peeled walnuts; 3 cloves of garlic; 1/2 teaspoon coarse sea salt; 2 crustless slices of white country bread; 2/3 cup extra-virgin olive oil; juice of 1 lemon*

method   Cut the swordfish into 1-inch cubes and place in an earthenware dish. Beat together the lemon juice and olive oil and add the paprika and plenty of salt and pepper. Pour this mixture over the swordfish, turning the cubes to coat them, and leave in a cool place to marinate for at least 4 hours, preferably overnight.

    Pour boiling water over the bay leaves and leave for 1 hour, then drain.

to make the sauce   Grind together the walnuts, garlic and salt until you have a paste. Traditionally this is done with a mortar and pestle; this method does achieve the best results, but the food processor is a quick alternative.

    Soak the bread briefly in water and squeeze dry. Using the back of a wooden spoon, combine the walnut paste with the bread. Mix together the olive oil and lemon juice, then slowly beat this emulsification into the walnut mixture, until you have a smooth sauce.

    When you are ready to cook the kabobs, have the charcoals just glowing or the broiler heated to medium. Thread 4 cubes of fish onto each kabob stick, interspersing with the fresh bay leaves.

    Cook the fish for 12 to 15 minutes, turning several times and basting frequently with the marinade. Serve with the *tarator* sauce and lemon quarters.

Grilled fish with egg-and-lemon sauce

Avgolémono, the famous Greek sauce of eggs and lemons, is thought to have originated among Byzantine cooks, but was eagerly adopted by the Ottoman court. In medieval cooking, eggs were regularly used to add richness; but what gives this sauce its unique quality is the sharpness of the lemon.

In Turkey today the sauce is known as *terbiye*, or "to behave" — a reference to the fact that, unless handled with care, the egg-based sauce will curdle. It can be served with grilled chicken or lamb; or stirred into chicken, vegetable or lamb stock for soup. But I like it best with simply grilled fish.

2 whole sea bass, mullet or large mackerel,
  about 1lb each, undrawn weight; sea salt;
1 lemon; 2 extra-large eggs plus the yolk of 1 extra-large egg;
juice of 1 1/2 large or 2 small lemons

method Draw the fish if the fish merchant has not already done so and wash well. With a sharp knife, make several deep slashes across the flesh on each side, down to the bone. Sprinkle generously with salt, inside and out, and place 2 slices of lemon in the cavity of each fish.

Either have the barbecue coals glowing or the broiler heated to maximum. (If using a barbecue, it is much simpler if you have a hand-held grill into which you can "sandwich" the fish, to prevent it sticking to the barbecue.) Cook the fish for 7 to 8 minutes on each side, until the skin is nicely black and bubbled up in places.

When the fish is cooked, take it off the heat and let it rest while you make the sauce — a matter of a minute or two, to be done at the last minute. Whisk together the eggs and egg yolk with a pinch of salt then whisk in the lemon juice. Place over medium-low heat and continue whisking. The mixture will first froth up, then start to thicken. If it looks like getting too hot, whip the pan off the heat or the sauce will curdle. As soon as the sauce emulsifies, dilute with a few drops of cold water before serving.

Sardines in grape leaves

The fresh anchovies from the Black Sea have become a staple on the northeastern Turkish coast. In winter they are baked on top of pilaf, in summer wrapped in grape leaves and briefly grilled over charcoal. The Black Sea anchovies are larger than those generally fished out of the Mediterranean and sardines make a good substitute.

This is a dish strictly for the barbecue — the grape leaves protect the tender flesh of the fish.

1 packet of grape leaves marinated in brine;
12 fresh sardines, scaled and drawn;
several good handfuls of fresh flat-leaf parsley,
  leaves finely chopped;
3 cloves of garlic, peeled and finely chopped;
2 lemons; sea salt and freshly ground black pepper;
olive oil

method Have the barbecue coals glowing. Rinse the grape leaves well — you need 12. Wash the fish and pat dry. Mix together the parsley and garlic. Slice the lemons finely — you need 12 slices.

Lay a grape leaf flat and place a sardine on it — the head and tail should just come over the edge. Stuff the cavity of the fish with some of the garlic and parsley mixture and poke in a slice of lemon. Season generously and dribble a little oil over — you don't need much because the sardine is an oily fish. Wrap up the fish in the leaf to make a bundle. Repeat with the remaining 11 fish.

Place the bundles on the glowing coals and cook for 4 to 5 minutes a side. The grape leaf will become black and shrivel — scrape it away before eating the sardines with your fingers.

Barbecued trout

Although the Ottomans did cook with sea fish, they were people of the land, where there was grazing for their horses, and so more familiar with the river fish of the mountains — the brown trout. Today, throughout Turkey, trout remains a popular fish, although the very best are said to come from the region of Erzurum. In summer there are restaurants dedicated to trout, usually set beside tinkling streams — I have even been to one where the trout swim along a channel of water in the bar where the bottles are cooled.

4 small trout; sea salt; olive oil; 2 lemons, quartered, to serve

method Have the barbecue coals glowing. Wash the trout well inside the cavity then pat dry. Sprinkle inside and out liberally with salt and rub a little olive oil into the flesh. With most fish it is advisable to make several deep slashes across the flesh, but this is not necessary with trout, whose skin becomes beautifully crisp on the barbecue. Simply place the fish on the barbecue, high above the coals, and grill for 5 to 6 minutes on each side, until the skin is bubbled in places, crisp and golden. Serve with the quarters of lemon and, preferably, a salad of fresh leaves.

note The mackerel is another Turkish favorite that also tastes at its very best cooked over charcoal, especially if freshly caught.

Shrimp guveç

Large shrimp in their shells are cooked directly on the barbecue, usually after a brief marinade in olive oil, lemon juice and garlic. Smaller shrimp often find their way into a little dish of vegetables, served bubbling hot and topped with cheese (typically a Turkish hard cheese, but Gruyère or Swiss make adequate substitutes). Traditionally, the little earthenware pots in which the shrimp are cooked, and which give the dish its name, were placed in the ashes of the fire or barbecue to cook.

2 tablespoons olive oil; 3 scallions, chopped;
1 small mild red chili pepper; 1 small mild green chili pepper;
2 cloves of garlic, peeled and finely chopped;
2 large field mushrooms, diced;
sea salt and freshly ground black pepper;
2 tomatoes, diced; a small handful each of fresh flat-leaf
    parsley and dill, leaves finely chopped;
7oz raw shrimp (tiger prawns work well), peeled;
Gruyère or Swiss cheese

method Heat the oil in a heavy skillet and fry the scallions, chili peppers, garlic and mushrooms for 3 to 4 minutes, stirring regularly. Add seasoning and the diced tomatoes and cook for another 3 to 4 minutes. Toss in the herbs, together with the shrimp, and cook for 1 minute longer, just until the shrimp turn pink. Take off the heat and divide the mixture between 4 small earthenware bowls. Top with grated cheese.

Heat the oven to 400°F. Bake the pots for 20 minutes, until the cheese melts and the mixture is bubbling. Serve straight away, still in the pots.

Ladies' thighs köfte

Not all kabobs and meatballs are grilled. So called because their round shape was likened to the thighs of a pleasantly plump woman, these fried meatballs were a court favorite.

1 large white onion, peeled and finely chopped;
3 tablespoons butter; 1/4 cup basmati rice, well rinsed;
1lb ground lamb;
sea salt and freshly ground black pepper;
1 heaped teaspoon allspice;
1 heaped teaspoon paprika;
a large handful of fresh flat-leaf parsley,
   leaves finely chopped;
1 large egg, beaten; all-purpose flour;
sunflower or peanut oil for frying;
1 lemon, quartered, to serve

method Cook the onion in the melted butter for 10 minutes until golden brown. Meanwhile, bring a pan of salted water to a boil and cook the rice for 5 minutes at an active boil, drain. Add half the ground lamb to the fried onions and continue to cook over medium heat for 2 to 3 minutes, stirring all the time, until the lamb is brown; let cool thoroughly.

To assemble the *köfte*, mix together the cooked lamb and onions with the remaining raw lamb. Season well and add the spices, parsley and drained rice. Stir in the egg thoroughly. Dust your hands with flour and break off nuggets of the mixture about the size of a small egg. Flatten each — and remember that the shape you are looking for is that of a plump lady's thigh.

Fill a deep skillet with oil to a depth of about 11/4 inches. Heat the oil to the stage where a cube of bread dipped in it just sizzles. Sprinkle a surface with flour and roll a few *köfte* at a time in it. Fry the *köfte* a few at a time for 2 to 3 minutes on each side, until golden brown. Drain on paper towels and serve piping hot with the wedges of lemon and perhaps a selection of salads.

Grilled green peppers with yogurt

You may be familiar with chunks of meat interspersed with peppers, onions and tomatoes on a kabob, but the reality is this approach usually leads to overcooked meat, undercooked onions and peppers and soggy tomatoes. Masters of the barbecue prefer to grill the vegetables individually. The absolute favorite are long, thin green bell peppers but halved onions and whole tomatoes are also put over the charcoal.

8 long green bell peppers; 3 tablespoons strained yogurt;
sea salt and freshly ground black pepper; paprika

method Have the charcoal glowing or heat the broiler to maximum. Place the peppers over the charcoal or under the broiler and cook for 2 to 3 minutes until lightly black on both sides (this can take up to 10 minutes on each side). As soon as they are cool enough to handle, peel off the papery skin. Arrange on a plate. Mix the yogurt with just enough water to thin it (1 tablespoon should do it) and pour over the peppers. It is important to do this while they are hot. Season generously with salt and pepper and then sprinkle the paprika over the yogurt. The peppers can be served straight away but are also good cold.

from the vegetable market

The Ottomans may have been great meat eaters, but today in the eastern Mediterranean countryside meat is for high days and holidays; the staple, everyday food of the region is based on vegetables, legumes and grains. The vegetables, of course, change with the seasons. Artichokes, fava beans and cardoons herald the arrival of spring; eggplants, zucchini, bell peppers and tomatoes are at their luscious best in early summer; pumpkins and vast cabbages, bright green pickling cucumbers and shiny piles of olives appear in the fall. There is rarely, though, a shortage of fresh herbs, garlic, onions and purple-tinged shallots. In the vegetable markets women bring the produce of their smallholding to earn a little spare cash, but also to have a chance of a gossip with their friends.

opposite *women at market, Kastamönu, Turkey*

Stuffed vegetables
The Ottomans aimed for food to taste of more than itself — by which I mean they liked to take a simple ingredient and through culinary embellishments turn it into an exquisite morsel. Sometimes this even took the form of chefs' jokes. They would take ground meat and shape it into the form of a lamb chop; hollow out a mackerel or an eggplant, stuff it with rice and nuts, and then serve it whole so the diner was taken by surprise when it was sliced.

There is, of course, no need to go to such elaborate lengths. But sometimes the act of stuffing a vegetable can transform ingredients in a way that cannot be achieved if they are cooked separately. A baked bell pepper served with rice and lamb does not taste the same as one that has been cooked with a rice stuffing.

These dishes generally taste best served warm, either an hour or so after cooking or gently reheated the next day. With bread and yogurt, they are sufficiently substantial to make a meal in their own right.

Stuffed cabbage leaves

This is usually made with a green cabbage that is known as *lahano*, which grows to vast size, but Savoy cabbage makes a good substitute.

1 medium lahano *or Savoy cabbage;*
2 tablespoons olive oil;
1 medium onion, peeled and finely chopped;
7oz ground lamb;
1/4 cup basmati rice, well rinsed;
a small handful each of fresh dill and fresh mint,
    leaves roughly chopped;
sea salt and freshly ground black pepper;
a generous pinch of allspice; chicken stock;
thick and creamy strained yogurt, to serve

method Pick the tough outer leaves off the cabbage and use them to line a heavy-bottomed pot. Carefully peel off 12 leaves, keeping them intact as far as possible. Bring a large pan of salted water to a boil and blanch the leaves for 2 minutes, then drain and plunge immediately into iced water; set aside.

Now make the filling for the cabbage leaves. Heat the oil in a heavy skillet over medium heat and add the onion. Fry for 10 minutes, stirring occasionally, until golden. Take off the heat and add the cooked onion to the raw ground meat and rice. Stir in the chopped herbs together with generous seasoning and the allspice. Briefly pound the mixture with a wooden spoon (you can also use your hands) and then divide the mixture into 12 balls of roughly equal size.

Take a cabbage leaf and cut out any tough stem. Fashion one of the balls of stuffing into a rough oblong shape and place it across the stem end of the cabbage. Fold each side of the cabbage leaf inward and then roll it up to form a cylinder shape. Place it, seam side down, in the pot lined with cabbage leaves. Repeat the process with the remaining leaves until you have 12 rolls.

Pour sufficient chicken stock over to barely cover the leaves then weigh them down with a layer of foil, followed by a plate. Slowly bring the stock to a simmer and then let cook for 45 minutes. Carefully pick out the cooked cabbage rolls and serve with the yogurt.

note   Stuffed cabbage leaves are also excellent served with *avgolémono* sauce. Beat the yolks of 2 eggs with the juice of 1 lemon then slowly whisk in some of the stock in which the leaves were cooked. Heat gently, stirring constantly, until thick, but do not allow to boil or there is a risk that the sauce will curdle.

Vegetable market, Syria

Stuffed eggplant

The eggplant is the king of vegetables across the Arab world but it is in Turkey where it really climbs onto the throne — it is often said that there are more than 200 traditional Turkish recipes for preparing eggplants, although I suspect in reality there are many more. But the absolute favorite is that known as *Imam Bayildi* or "the imam swooned" — whether with delight or from excessive eating has never been made clear. Although the Turks today claim it as their own, so, too, do the Syrians and the Lebanese, and I have even seen a suggestion in a Greek cook book that the dish was invented in Greece by a local pasha who wanted to impress his imam. What is certain is that it was a favorite dish across the Ottoman Empire and remains so today, not just in the Middle East, but in Europe as well.

serves 4 as an appetizer or 2 as a main course   *2 eggplants, about 6 inches long; 1 cup olive oil;*
4 small or 2 large white onions, about 1lb in total, peeled and chopped into fine half moons;
2 cloves of garlic, peeled and finely chopped;
1 teaspoon sweet paprika;
freshly ground black pepper; sea salt;
3 tablespoons finely chopped fresh flat-leaf parsley;
2 tablespoons tomato paste;
1 long green Turkish pepper; 1 large tomato

method   Slice the eggplants in half lengthwise, retaining the stem. Scoop out the seeds in the middle of each half, leaving a rim of 1/2 to 3/4 inch of eggplant flesh all around and at the bottom. Heat the oven to 400°F.

Pour 2/3 cup of the oil into a pan in which the eggplants fit comfortably and place the pan over medium heat. It is very important the oil is thoroughly hot before you add the eggplants or they will absorb too much oil. When the oil is nearly smoking (which will take several minutes), add the eggplants flesh side down, standing well back as they might spit. Fry over medium heat for 10 to 15 minutes, turning several times, until the flesh of the eggplant is light brown and tender. Remove from the pan, being careful not to break the skin, and pat dry on paper towel. Place on a baking tray, flesh side up.

to make the filling   Heat the remaining oil in a separate skillet over low heat. When the oil is hot, add the onions and fry gently for 10 minutes, stirring regularly. Now add the chopped garlic and continue to fry gently for 10 minutes longer, still stirring regularly, until the onions are golden and the garlic tender. Add the sweet paprika, black pepper and salt to the pan and cook for 1 minute, then stir in the parsley and tomato paste. Let cook for 5 minutes longer, stirring occasionally.

Pile the onion mixture into the scooped-out middle of the eggplants. Cut the green pepper into 4 thin strips and place one lengthwise on top of the onion mixture in the halved eggplants. Cut 4 thin slices of tomato and place on top of the strip of green pepper. Transfer the baking tray to the heated oven and cook for 15 minutes, until the tomato and pepper are cooked. Let cool before serving.

variation   In southern Turkey, just over the water from the Greek islands, mint, oregano and basil sometimes replace the parsley in the filling and the paprika, spice of the Balkans, is replaced by ground coriander seeds for an altogether more Mediterranean taste.

Stuffed white zucchini with pomegranate and egg sauce

Traditionally, stuffed vegetables such as zucchini are braised, but I find it easier to bake them in individual foil packages in the oven. That way, if you do break the skin during the tricky business of hollowing out and stuffing the vegetable, at least the filling won't spill out during cooking. The sauce served here is similar to the famous Greek *avgolémono*, but in southeastern Turkey it is made sharp with pomegranate rather than lemon juice.

6 white zucchini; 8oz ground lamb;
2 tablespoons cooked garbanzo beans, drained;
3 fat cloves of garlic, peeled and finely chopped;
a small handful of fresh dill, finely chopped;
a small handful of fresh flat-leaf parsley, finely chopped;
sea salt and freshly ground black pepper; extra-virgin olive oil;
3 egg yolks; juice of 1 pomegranate;
3 to 4 tablespoons water

method Using an apple corer and a sharp knife, carefully hollow out the zucchini, first removing the stem end. This is a fiddly business — try not to split the skin and don't worry if you have to leave quite a bit of pulp inside. Your aim is to have a hollow tube to stuff; discard the pulp.

to make the stuffing Mix together the ground lamb, garbanzo beans, garlic and herbs and season well. Carefully stuff the zucchini, taking care not to press too hard or you will split the skin.

Heat the oven to 350°F. Cut off squares of foil to fit each zucchini, lay the zucchini on these and dribble with oil and salt. Wrap them up well and place them in the oven. Bake for 50 minutes to 1 hour, until soft.

Take the zucchini out of their foil and lay in a serving dish. Beat together the eggs and pomegranate juice and heat gently with the 3 to 4 tablespoons water (but do not boil or the eggs will curdle). Pour this sauce over the zucchini before serving.

Stuffed green peppers

1/2 cup long-grain rice (preferably basmati), rinsed and
*   drained; 1 large white onion, peeled and finely chopped;*
13oz ground lamb;
3 cloves of garlic, peeled and finely chopped;
1 teaspoon sea salt; freshly ground black pepper;
a good pinch of saffron strands;
1/2 teaspoon ground cinnamon;
a large handful of fresh flat-leaf parsley, leaves
*   finely chopped;*
10 small, thin-skinned green peppers or 5 large bell peppers;
5 or 6 grape leaves, rinsed; 3 cups water;
2 tablespoons tomato paste

method Heat the oven to 350°F. Mix the rice with the onion, lamb, garlic, salt, a generous quantity of pepper, the saffron, cinnamon and parsley. Cut off the tops of the peppers (but do not throw them away), remove the cores and seeds, being careful not to break the flesh. Stuff the rice and meat mixture into the cavities.

Choose a pot, preferably earthenware for best flavor, into which all the peppers will just fit standing upright. Line the bottom of the pot with the grape leaves, then carefully put in the peppers. Mix together the water and tomato paste then pour the mixture into the pot, making sure some of the liquid goes into the peppers. Replace the tops of the peppers (don't worry about a perfect match) then put foil over the top. Finally, put on the lid and place the pot in the middle of the heated oven.

Bake the peppers for about 2 hours, lifting up the lid and foil halfway through to baste them with the cooking liquid. Let cool in the pot; they are at their best served just warm, an hour or two after cooking, but can also be reheated or served cold.

variation For a vegetarian version from Greece, substitute pine nuts for the meat, leave out the saffron, but add some allspice, and replace the parsley with fresh dill and mint.

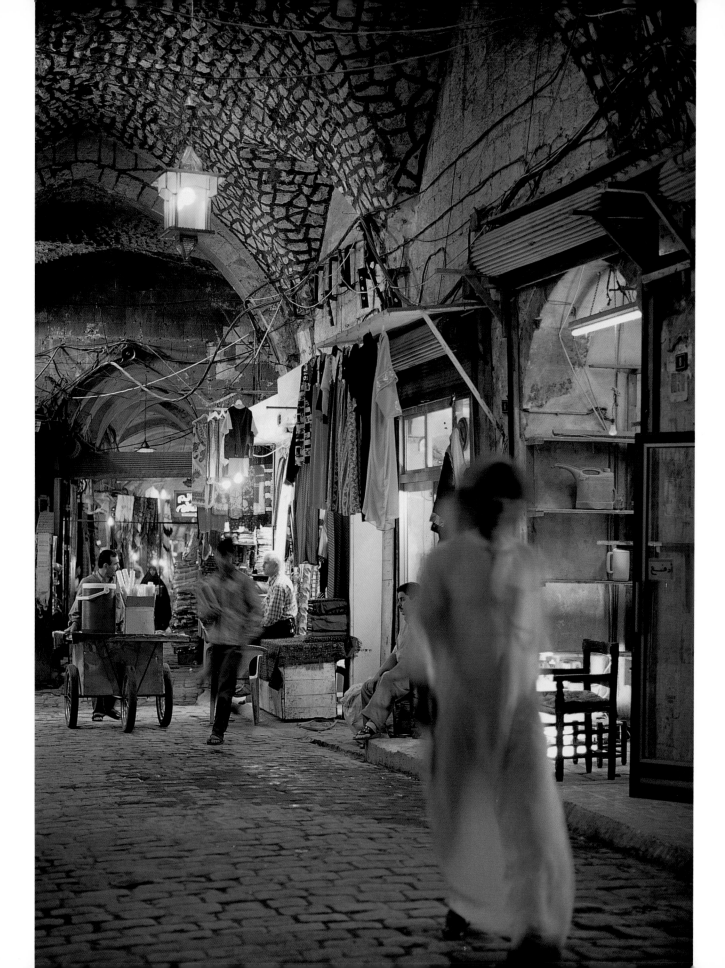

Bazaars and markets

The bazaar of my memories is a cool, dark place, the air heavy with the scent of spices, the space filled with the cries of the vendors, the gloom pierced by occasional shafts of sunlight darting through the grimy skylights of the barrel-vaulted roof. The narrow alleyways between stalls are packed with eager shoppers, occasionally pried apart by urgent deliverymen pushing their wares before them. It is a place to get lost in, to wander from well-defined section to section, to watch the copper beaters in one, barter with the spice merchants in another, tantalize yourself over fine fabrics or rich gold jewelry in a third. Above all it is a place redolent of the magic and mystery of the East.

Constantinople was famed for its markets, for all the goods of the vast Ottoman Empire ended up here to be traded. The small domed building down by the water's edge is still known to inhabitants of the city as the *Misir Çarsisi*, or Egyptian Market, after the exotic goods from the lands of the Nile that once arrived here by ship.

Today it has become something of a tourist attraction, although you can still find henna and aphrodisiacs, caviar and green tea, and fragrant heaps of spices. In the streets behind, on the hill leading up to the vast *Kapali Çarsi* or Covered Market, you will still find traditional craftsmen at work, beating copper and silver. But for a real flavor of the East you should travel farther, to Aleppo and Damascus in Syria, perhaps, or even as far as Cairo. It is easy here to imagine the Armenians and Jews who were the main traders of the Ottoman Empire haggling over exotic goods for the ever-hungry capital.

The market at Bursa, at the center of one of Turkey's most fertile regions, has a special place in my heart. On a fall visit there were piles of chestnuts to be made into delicate puddings, down-covered quince to be simmered in syrup, heaped piles of cucumbers and peppers for preserving, long bunches of purple grapes and plump figs. A return in late spring brought trays of lightly blushed peaches and apricots, bright, shiny cherries, crisp fava bean pods and tight little peas. No wonder the meat market was doing little business — the vegetables and fruit were simply too good to ignore.

previous pages left: *Lebanon;* **top right**: *Kas, Turkey;* **bottom right**: *Dalyan, Turkey* **opposite from left** *Bursa, Turkey; Beirut; Kalkan, Turkey* **above** *Edirne, Turkey*

Vegetables cooked in olive oil

Butter was the fat of choice for much Ottoman cooking, in legacy to their origins as nomadic herdsmen. But with an empire ringing the eastern Mediterranean, with its ancient olive groves, oil also had a part to play. The Ottomans particularly treasured Greek olive oil, and from the habits of the islanders they first learned to cook their vegetables slowly in oil. In these days when most vegetables are served crisp and crunchy, it is easy to forget the pleasures of melting, tender vegetables served very much on their own in their own fruity, oily cooking juices.

Artichokes in olive oil

4 large fresh globe artichokes; 3 lemons; 2 large carrots;
2 medium red potatoes;
8 tablespoons olive oil; a generous pinch of white sugar;
a generous pinch of sea salt; 2 fresh bay leaves;
1 tablespoon chopped fresh dill fronds

method   Prepare the artichokes by first peeling the stems and then cutting off the tough end and removing any small leaves. Cut one of the lemons in half and rub the peeled stem with the cut face to prevent discoloring.

Now remove the hearts from the artichokes, beginning by snapping off the outer leaves — they should break off at the bottom. With a sharp knife, cut across the artichoke just above the choke and immediately rub the cut surface with the cut lemon. Now use the knife to remove any remaining hairy choke. Use a peeler to scrape off the bottom of any remaining dark leaves. Squeeze the juice of the remaining half of lemon into a bowl of cold water and place each heart in this as soon as it is ready.

When all the hearts are prepared, peel the carrots and potatoes and cut their flesh into bite-size pieces — they should not be too small or they will disintegrate during cooking. Choose a heavy pan with a tight-fitting lid, into which all the artichoke hearts will fit, and pack them in cut side down, so that the stems stick up. Scatter the diced potato and carrot over them; then pour in the olive oil and the juice of the 2 remaining lemons. Add sugar and salt, the bay leaves and, finally, enough water to generously cover the bottom of the artichoke hearts — the liquid should come about halfway up the stems.

Cover the top of the pan with foil and then the lid, then place over medium heat. Simmer for 45 to 50 minutes — during this time resist the temptation to peer under the foil or you will lose the steam. Now take the artichokes out and place in a serving dish. Turn the heat up under the liquid and boil hard for 10 minutes or so, until the liquid reduces. Pour the carrots, potatoes and juice over the artichokes and let cool. Before serving, check seasoning and sprinkle with fresh dill.

note   In season, fresh green peas can also be added to the mix, cooked with the carrots and potatoes for the last 10 minutes of boiling.

Olives, Dalyan, Turkey

Baby whole fava beans in olive oil

This Greek treatment makes the most of fava beans, serving the whole pod rather than just the shiny green bean inside. For best effects you need to use very fresh, crisp and very small pods.

1lb fresh young fava beans in their pods,
 the smaller the better;
1 teaspoon sea salt; juice of 1 lemon;
1 teaspoon white sugar;
4 large scallions, chopped, including green parts;
a good handful of fresh dill, stems removed
 and fronds chopped;
1 teaspoon dried mint; freshly ground black pepper;
1/2 teaspoon allspice; 6 tablespoons extra-virgin olive oil;
scant 1 cup water

method Wash the fava beans well and cut off their stems. Carefully remove the string that runs down the side of each bean. Sprinkle the whole beans with the salt, lemon juice and sugar and let stand for about 15 minutes.

Now place half of the beans in a heavy-bottomed Dutch oven in which they will all fit. Layer the scallions, half the dill and mint and a generous seasoning of pepper. Sprinkle the allspice over. Lay the remaining beans on top and scatter the rest of the herbs over. Add the oil and the water. Bring to a boil, turn down to a slow simmer and let cook for about 11/2 hours — or until the beans are meltingly tender.

Let cool a little before serving; this dish is usually served just warm, along with lots of thick, creamy yogurt spiked with a little garlic and more dried mint.

Green beans in olive oil with tomato sauce

11/2lbs long green or runner beans;
4 or 5 tomatoes, about 1lb in total, peeled and seeded;
1 large white onion, peeled;
5 tablespoons olive oil; 2 teaspoons white sugar;
1 teaspoon sea salt; 21/2 tablespoons tomato paste

method Top and tail the beans, wash well and cut each across into 3 pieces. Roughly chop the tomatoes and cut the onion in half. Heat the oil in a large, deep pan over medium heat and add the tomatoes, sugar, salt, tomato paste and onion. Cook for 10 minutes or so, stirring from time to time, until you have a thick sauce. Now add the beans, together with sufficient water to barely cover. Cover the pan with foil, followed by a lid, and cook over a low heat for 45 minutes or so, until the beans are tender. Let cool; this is a dish that tastes much better reheated.

Leeks in olive oil with rice

6 large leeks, about 3lbs in total;
2 medium carrots, peeled;
2/3 cup olive oil; 3 fat cloves of garlic, peeled;
4 teaspoons white sugar; 1 teaspoon sea salt;
a few sprigs of fresh parsley;
2 level tablespoons basmati rice, well-rinsed;
juice of 1/2 lemon; freshly ground black pepper;
a good handful of fresh flat-leaf parsley, finely chopped

method Trim the green ends and the stems from the leeks then cut the white part across diagonally at roughly 11/2 inch intervals — you should end up with 4 or 5 pieces per leek. Rinse well under cold running water, then drain. Cut the carrots in half across and then into quarters vertically.

Heat the oil in a heavy-bottomed Dutch oven over medium heat and add the leeks and carrots, together with the whole cloves of garlic. Cook for 15 minutes, stirring several times, until both leeks and carrots are lightly browned. Now add the sugar, salt, parsley and rice and stir well to coat the rice with the oil. Add barely enough water to cover, bring to a boil and then turn down to a simmer. Cover the pot with foil and then a lid and let cook over low heat for 10 minutes. Turn off the heat and let stand for 10 minutes longer before taking off the lid. Serve at room temperature, dressed with lemon juice, seasoned with pepper and scattered with parsley.

Guveç dishes

The *guveç* is the name given to a pot in which the long-cooked casseroles were both cooked and served. Typically made of earthenware, it would be sealed and buried in the ashes of the fire and often left overnight, although the fading heat of the bakers' oven was also used. Just as the *tagine* did in Morocco, the *guveç* has lent its name to a particular kind of dish, of vegetables, legumes and even fruit cooked slowly with small amounts of meat. In fact, the use of fruit with meat may well have been adopted from the Caliphate of the Moors, brought over by the many Spanish Jews who moved to Constantinople.

Eggplant and lamb guveç

This summer *guveç* is similar to a ratatouille with the embellishment of a little meat.

The addition of honey and thyme is a Greek touch, but the use of butter instead of olive oil is firmly Turkish. The fat gives the tomato sauce a slick finish.

*2 medium eggplants, about 1lb in total;
sea salt; 4 tablespoons unsalted butter;
1 large onion, peeled and finely chopped; 8oz lamb,
preferably cut from shoulder or leg, trimmed of fat
and cut into small pieces; sunflower or vegetable oil;
1 red bell pepper; 1 green bell pepper;
1 fresh red chili pepper (optional); 3 large beefsteak tomatoes,
washed and quartered; 1 tablespoon honey;
2 tablespoons water; several sprigs of fresh thyme;
a handful of fresh flat-leaf parsley, leaves finely chopped*

method Cut the eggplants into quarters lengthwise and then cut each slice across at regular intervals of about 11/4 inches. Sprinkle generously with salt and let drain in a colander for about 30 minutes to remove any bitter juices.

Meanwhile, melt half the butter in a heavy-bottomed pan and add the onion. Fry over medium heat, stirring occasionally, for 8 to 10 minutes, until the onion is soft and golden. Now add the meat and fry briefly for another couple of minutes, stirring all the time, until the small pieces are nicely brown; remove and set aside.

Rinse the eggplant with plenty of water and drain well. Fill a skillet with oil to a depth of roughly 3/4 inch and place over medium heat. When the oil is very hot (important — otherwise the eggplant will absorb too much oil) add about a quarter of the eggplant pieces. Fry the eggplant briefly in batches until lightly golden, lifting out with a draining spoon and draining on paper towels.

To prepare the peppers, first slice off the top with the stem and remove the core, including any seeds. Slice the flesh vertically into thin strips. Do the same for the chili if you are using it.

When all the eggplant is cooked, return your heavy-bottomed pan to medium heat and add the remaining butter. Hurl in the sliced peppers and cook, stirring, for 5 minutes or so, until soft. Now add the quartered tomatoes, a good sprinkling of salt, the honey and the 2 tablespoons of water. Cook, stirring all the time, for several minutes, until the tomatoes start to break down.

Return the meat and onions to the pan and add the fried eggplant together with the sprigs of thyme. A few grinds of black pepper will also not go amiss at this stage. Turn the heat down to low, cover and let simmer gently for 15 to 20 minutes, until the meat is nicely tender. Do not be tempted to cook for too long or the eggplant will disintegrate — you want it to stay in distinct chunks.

Now check that the seasoning is to your satisfaction and take the pan off the heat. Stir in a generous quantity of fresh parsley and let stand for at least 20 minutes or so before serving.

Harvesting sugar beets, central Anatolia

Figs, grapes and almonds with lamb

8 shallots, peeled; 4 tablespoons unsalted butter;
13oz lamb (shoulder or leg), trimmed of fat
    and cut into small pieces;
8 plump dried figs, quartered; 1 cup whole almonds;
sea salt and freshly ground black pepper;
1 tablespoon honey; 2 bay leaves;
about 21/4 cups lamb or chicken stock;
7oz black grapes, halved and seeded

method   Heat the oven to 300°F.

Break any shallots that have them into cloves, otherwise leave whole. Melt two-thirds of the butter in a heavy skillet over low heat. Add the shallots and brown them slowly for 10 minutes, turning regularly.

With a draining spoon, lift the browned shallots out of the pan and place in a Dutch oven, preferably earthenware for the best flavor. Return the skillet to the heat, adding the remaining knob of butter. Turn up the heat and briefly fry the meat in 2 batches, until lightly browned — a minute or two, stirring. Lift the meat out and add it to the shallots, together with the figs and the whole almonds. Season well; then pour in the honey, stirring well to coat the meat. Finally, poke in the bay leaves.

Warm the stock and pour into the Dutch oven — there should be enough to barely cover the contents. Cover the pot and place in the heated oven. Let cook for 11/2 hours, until the meat is melting tender. Take out of the oven, add the grapes and leave for at least 30 minutes before serving; this also reheats well.

Legumes, Egyptian Bazaar, Istanbul, Turkey

Garbanzo and quince with lamb

2 tablespoons unsalted butter;

1 small white onion, peeled and finely chopped;

1 large carrot, peeled and finely chopped;

1 large clove of garlic, peeled and finely chopped;

1 large quince; 7oz lamb (shoulder or leg),
   trimmed of fat and cut into small pieces;

13oz canned garbanzo beans, drained and rinsed;

1 tablespoon chopped fresh dill;

sea salt and freshly ground black pepper;

1/2 cup chopped walnuts;

3 tablespoons concentrated grape syrup (if you can't find
   grape syrup, use red-wine vinegar sweetened
   with 1 heaped teaspoon sugar)

method Melt the butter and add the onion, carrot and garlic. Fry slowly, stirring occasionally, for 10 to 15 minutes, until the vegetables are tender but not brown. Meanwhile, peel the quince (this should be done at the last minute to prevent discoloring) and chop the flesh into bite-size pieces.

Now turn up the heat to medium and add the lamb pieces. Fry for 3 to 4 minutes, stirring, until the meat is lightly brown. Add the pieces of quince, the garbanzo beans, dill (reserving a little to sprinkle over the dish at the end), a generous amount of seasoning, the walnuts and the grape syrup. Stir all together well and add just enough water to cover — about 21/4 cups.

Bring to a boil, turn down to a simmer and let bubble gently for 45 to 50 minutes, until the quince and lamb are both tender. Let stand for 10 minutes before serving, sprinkled with the remaining dill.

Baked okra
with tomatoes and peppers

The French name for okra is *cornes de Grècque* ("Greek horns") and certainly this dish of okra, arranged like roof tiles with their topping of peppers and tomatoes, has its origins in Greek culinary tradition. But then for centuries the Greeks were vastly important to the Ottoman Empire, especially as administrators, and long comprised a significant element of Constantinople's population.

11/2lbs okra; make sure they are not woody,
     by pinching them between finger and thumb —
     they should feel soft;
7oz white-wine vinegar; sea salt;
3 tablespoons olive oil for frying;
2 white onions, peeled and finely chopped;
4 large tomatoes;
2 green peppers, preferably Turkish thin-skinned;
2 red peppers (the long, thin Italian variety are ideal);
a generous handful of flat-leaf parsley,
     finely chopped;
freshly ground black pepper;
scant 1/2 cup extra-virgin olive oil;
scant 1/2 cup water

method   Wash the okra briefly and dry well. Trim off the end of the stems, but take care not to actually cut into the pod. Put the okra in a large, flat dish and sprinkle the vinegar together with a generous quantity of salt over. Turn once or twice to coat and leave for about 45 minutes.

Meanwhile, heat the oven to 350°F. Heat the olive oil for frying and add the onions; fry, stirring occasionally, over medium heat for 10 to 15 minutes, until tinged golden brown.

Rinse the okra well. Choose a large, square and oven-proof earthenware dish and arrange the okra over the bottom — you will find they fit better if you arrange them in rows rather than succumbing to the temptation to simply throw them in. Cut each tomato into 4 or 5 slices across, discarding the ends, and lay across the okra.

Remove the stem and seeds from the red and green peppers, then cut the flesh into thin strips; crisscross these over the tomatoes. Scatter the parsley over. Season with plenty of pepper, but go easy on the salt because the okra will have retained some. Finally pour in the oil, shaking to distribute evenly, and add the water. Transfer the dish to the hot oven.

Bake for an hour or so — the exact cooking time depends on the size and freshness of the okra. Toward the end of cooking, pick one out to taste; it should be soft, but not falling apart. Let cool in its own juices and serve barely warm. The dish tastes even better the next day.

rich pilafs and rural breads

The Turkic peoples, nomadic horsemen from the steppes, lived on a diet of mare's milk and rice, perhaps with a little fresh horse's blood to spice up their meals; and when the Ottoman armies marched it was often remarked that they only seemed to need rice to sustain them. Rice has always been the food of preference for the Turkish peoples and with the pilaf they developed a most sophisticated way of cooking the grain.

The chefs of the Ottoman court produced ever richer pilafs, laden with nuts, rich with butter, scented and colored with expensive saffron. Very often meat, whether chicken livers or ground lamb, was added to the pilafs to make them more substantial. Many of the pilafs popular in Turkey today retain the name of the sultan under whose reign they were introduced; there is even one named after the Palace of Topkapi itself.

cooking pilafs This way of preparing rice, probably learned from the Persians, gives it a unique texture and subtlety; to this day Turkish pilafs are admired across the Middle Eastern world. Pilafs are also popular in Greece, where dried currants and raisins are often added in place of the nuts typically used in Turkey. In Anatolia and Armenia, and across the Balkans, pilafs are also made with bulgur wheat.

Use long-grain rice, but not the presteamed variety — I favor basmati. Before cooking the rice, soak it in plenty of water for at least 30 minutes, then drain and rinse well. The aim is to remove excess starch, so the cooked grains don't stick together. While the rice is cooking, resist any temptation to stir; nor should you skimp on the final 10 to 15 minutes or so resting under a clean dish towel. If you have guests and don't want to be fiddling around at the last moment, simply extend this stage to up to 45 minutes — the pilaf will taste just as good tepid. The textures and delicate, spicy flavors are the important things.

Pilaf with chicken livers

6 tablespoons butter; 1 tablespoon olive oil;
1 onion, peeled and finely chopped; 1 tablespoon pine nuts;
2 tablespoons slivered almonds; 8oz chicken livers,
*   finely chopped; 11/4 cups long-grain rice, preferably*
*   basmati, soaked, rinsed and drained;*
2 tablespoons dried currants; 1 teaspoon paprika;
21/2 cups water; salt and pepper;
a generous handful of fresh flat-leaf parsley, finely chopped

method Melt half the butter with the oil in a large, heavy-bottomed skillet with a lid over low heat. Add the onion and sweat slowly for 10 minutes, until soft but not colored. Now turn up the heat to medium and add the pine nuts, almonds and chicken livers. Fry for 5 minutes longer, stirring constantly, until the nuts are lightly browned and the livers cooked through.

Melt the remaining butter in the pan and add the rice, currants and paprika. Cook slowly for 3 to 4 minutes, stirring all the time, to make sure all the rice is coated in fat. Bring the measured water to a boil, pour into the rice, season well, stir just once and cover. Leave to cook for 12 to 15 minutes over low heat, until all the water is absorbed. During this time, resist the temptation to remove the lid.

Take the rice off the heat and carefully stir in the chicken liver and nut mixture. Cover with a clean dish towel and replace the lid. Leave off the heat for 10 to 15 minutes. Fluff the rice up with a fork, sprinkle with the parsley and serve.

Spice bazaar, Istanbul, Turkey

Eggplant pilaf

2 large eggplants, about 1lb in total;
sea salt; 3 tablespoons unsalted butter;
1 large onion, peeled and finely chopped;
3 cloves of garlic, peeled and finely chopped;
1 cup long-grain rice, preferably basmati,
   soaked, rinsed and drained;
1 teaspoon white sugar; freshly ground black pepper;
1/2 teaspoon coriander seeds; 2 cloves;
1 stick of cinnamon;
4 teaspoons paprika paste (or failing that tomato
   paste mixed with paprika);
41/2 cups chicken stock; sunflower oil

method Peel the eggplants in strips lengthwise at intervals, giving them a striped effect. Cut them across at regular intervals and then cut each slice into 4 quarters, so you have bite-size pieces. Sprinkle generously with sea salt and let drain in a colander, pressed down with a plate or other weight.

In a heavy skillet over a medium heat, melt 2 tablespoons of the butter and add the onion and garlic. Cook, stirring occasionally, for 10 minutes or so, until golden.

Now add the rice, together with the remaining butter, and stir well to make sure all the grains are coated with fat. Also add the sugar, some salt and a generous grinding of pepper, the spices and finally the paprika paste. Again, stir well, then pour in the stock. Bring to a boil, turn down to a simmer and let cook for 10 to 12 minutes, until small holes appear in the surface.

Meanwhile, cook the eggplant. Fill a skillet with the sunflower oil to a depth of 3/4 inch and warm the oil until it is nearly spitting. Rinse the eggplant of salt and pat dry. Fry it in several batches, taking care never to overcrowd the pan, until it is golden. Remove with a draining spoon and drain on paper towel.

When the rice is ready, carefully stir in the fried eggplant, cover with a cloth and leave to stand for 10 to 15 minutes. Fluff the rice up with a fork before serving.

variation In summer, fresh cherries are sometimes used instead of eggplants. Make the pilaf as in the above recipe, leaving out the paprika paste, and simply substituting the cherries for the fried eggplant. Do, though, be careful to warn your fellow diners about the pits.

previous pages right *shepherds and their flock beneath Mount Ararat, eastern Turkey*

Topkapi pilaf

The kitchens at the Topkapi Palace in Istanbul give a clue to the excesses that marked the latter days of the Ottoman Empire. The chimneys on their ten-domed buildings sit squatly above the second courtyard, opposite the harem. In the kitchens there are huge cauldrons, so vast it took four men to lift them. I like to imagine the cauldrons being used to make this type of richly scented pilaf that the sultans were reputedly so fond of.

4 tablespoons butter; 1 tablespoon olive oil;
a large bunch of scallions, finely chopped, including
*   the tender green parts;*
1/2 cup whole, unskinned almonds;
2 tablespoons pine nuts; 1/2 teaspoon ground cinnamon;
2/3 cup small, dried black currants;
21/2 cups chicken stock;
11/4 cups long-grain rice, preferably
*   basmati, soaked, rinsed and drained;*
6 black peppercorns; 3 cloves;
a good pinch of saffron strands; salt;
1 tablespoon finely chopped fresh flat-leaf parsley

method Melt half the butter with the oil in a large, heavy-bottomed skillet with a lid over medium heat. Add the scallions and sweat slowly for 2 minutes, until soft. Now turn up the heat and add the almonds and pine nuts. Fry for another 3 to 4 minutes, stirring constantly, until the nuts are lightly brown. Take off the heat and stir in the cinnamon and currants.

Heat the chicken stock to just below boiling. Melt the remaining butter in the pan and, when it is foaming, add the rice. Stir well to make sure all the rice is coated in fat then add the peppercorns, cloves and saffron. Pour the hot chicken stock into the rice and add salt to taste, depending on the saltiness of the stock. Stir just once. Bring to a boil and reduce to a simmer for 10 to 12 minutes, until all the stock is absorbed and small holes appear on the surface.

Take the rice off the heat and carefully fold in the onion, currant and nut mixture. Cover with a clean towel and then the lid. Leave off the heat for 10 to 15 minutes — do not remove the lid during this time. Fluff the rice up with a fork and sprinkle with the parsley before serving.

variation Another classic pilaf from Ottoman times is named after one of the greatest of sultans, Suleyman the Magnificent. The approach is the same as for Topkapi pilaf, but small pieces of lamb are added to the rice together with the raisins and almonds and the saffron and pine nuts are left out.

Bulgur wheat pilaf

Much of the rice consumed in Turkey was once imported from Iran, just about the only part of the eastern Mediterranean the Ottomans did not get their hands on at some point. The high upland plains of the heartland did not lend themselves to the cultivation of rice, but they were ideal for wheat and it is this that has always been the staple grain. The simplest bulgur wheat pilaf was dressed with nothing more than butter but a few vegetables make it into a meal in itself, and one that can be transported into the fields for a picnic. You might, however, prefer to serve it with grilled meats.

4 tablespoons unsalted butter; 1 large white onion, peeled and
finely chopped; 31/2 cups chicken or lamb stock;
scant 2 cups coarse-grain bulgur wheat, rinsed and drained;
2 green bell peppers, cored and diced;
2 large beefsteak tomatoes, peeled, seeded and diced;
sea salt and freshly ground black pepper

method   Melt 21/2 tablespoons of the butter in a heavy skillet over medium heat and add the onion. Fry for 15 minutes or so, stirring from time to time, until the onion is nicely golden. Meanwhile, heat the stock.

Add the remaining knob of butter and the bulgur to the pan and cook, stirring all the time, for 3 to 4 minutes. Now add the diced peppers and tomatoes and cook for another 2 or 3 minutes, still stirring. Season generously, particularly with salt, then pour the hot stock over. Bring to a boil then turn down to an active simmer and let cook for 10 minutes or so, until all the stock is absorbed and small holes start to appear in the surface of the wheat. Do not be tempted to stir during this stage. Take the pilaf off the heat and cover with a clean towel. Let stand for 15 minutes or so then, with a fork, fluff it up, starting from the outside of the pan. Leave, again covered with the towel, for another 5 to 10 minutes before serving.

Harvesting wheat in Kurdistan

Pilaf with mussels

One of the favorite dishes of the Ottoman court was mussels individually stuffed with a spicy rice and nut mixture. Delicious, but deeply impractical unless (improbably) you have staff in your kitchen. This version provides the flavors, although perhaps with less elegance.

2 tablespoons olive oil;
2 white onions, peeled and finely chopped;
3/4 cup long-grain rice, preferably basmati,
*   soaked, rinsed and drained;*
1 tablespoon pine nuts; 1 tablespoon dried currants;
1/2 teaspoon allspice; 1 teaspoon ground cinnamon;
sea salt and freshly ground black pepper; 1/3 cup water;
1 large tomato, peeled and finely chopped;
30 to 35 large fresh mussels in their shells

Tyre, Lebanon

method Heat the oil in a heavy pan large enough to cook the pilaf and add the onions. Cook slowly over medium heat, stirring occasionally, for 10 minutes or so, until lightly golden. Now add the rice, pine nuts, currants, allspice, cinnamon and generous seasoning. Stir all well together for several minutes, the aim being to coat all the grains of rice with oil. Then add the water and the chopped tomato. Let cook slowly for 10 minutes or so until all the water is absorbed. During this stage you can stir the rice mixture occasionally to prevent it from sticking.

Meanwhile, prepare the mussels. First scrub them clean on the outside then debeard them, pulling off the small strands that stick out from the side. Discard any mussels with broken shells or that do not tap when closed. Leave the cleaned mussels under running water.

When the rice is dry, take it off the heat and flatten the top. Arrange the mussels all over the surface in a concentric pattern — they should completely cover the rice. Add another 7oz water. Cover with foil, then place a plate on top and finally the lid. Place over low heat and let cook for 20 minutes, resisting any temptation to lift the lid and take a peak.

Now remove the lid, plate and foil. All the mussels should have opened in the steam — discard any that haven't. Cover with a clean towel and let stand for 10 minutes or so before serving.

variation Along Turkey's Black Sea coast a pilaf made with fresh anchovies is very popular. As with the mussels, the anchovies are laid on top of the partially cooked pilaf, but in this case finished in the oven rather than steamed.

above *breadsellers in Damascus, Syria (left) and Istanbul, Turkey (right)* **opposite** *preparing bread, Turkey*

Bread

The making of the round, flat, thin village bread of the eastern Mediterranean is an art that must be perfected early in life. Certainly I have seen very young girls join in the garrulous group of women who frequently gather together for the task. Each takes a small piece of dough and rolls it out to paper thinness, using a long, wooden pole. There may be as many as ten women working together — but usually only one in charge of the upturned dome of metal over burning wood on which the bread is cooked. The rolled-out dough is deftly draped over the wooden pole and passed over to the chief cook, who puts it swiftly on to the hot, greased surface, flipping it over as soon as it starts to bubble and brown. Within a minute, the sheet of bread is cooked and transferred to a growing pile in the corner. If you are lucky enough to tear off a piece while it is still hot, I can guarantee that you will not forget the taste.

Lahmacun

This snack, Kurdish in origin, should really be cooked in a wood-fired oven, alongside the *pide* that are sometimes described as Turkish pizzas. But a passable effort can be made at home and the dough is very easy to make.

makes 4

for the dough *2 1/2 cups plain bread flour;*
1/4oz (2 1/4 teaspoons) instant dried yeast; 1 teaspoon salt;
1 teaspoon white sugar; 1 to 1 1/4 cups warm water

for the filling *7oz finely ground lamb;*
1/2 red onion, peeled and finely chopped;
1 large mild fresh red chili, seeds removed,
    finely chopped;
1 heaped teaspoon paprika;
4 teaspoons paprika paste; 1/2 teaspoon salt

to serve *1/2 red onion, peeled and chopped into fine*
    half moons; 1 teaspoon sumac (if available);
a large handful of fresh flat-leaf parsley, leaves
    roughly chopped; 2 lemons

method To make the dough, mix together the flour, yeast, salt and sugar. Make a well in the middle and slowly pour in about 2/3 cup of the warm water. Mix quickly with a wooden spoon and then continue adding just enough water to make a dough. Work quickly with your hands for a couple of minutes, until smooth and pliable, cover with a cloth and leave in a warm place for 45 minutes or so to rise.

Meanwhile, make the meat topping by simply mixing together all the ingredients. The texture should be smooth, almost pastelike — this is achieved most easily with a quick whizz in the food processor.

Heat the oven to 425°F. Divide the dough into 4 balls and, on a floured surface, roll each out thinly — one book of mine describes the dough as having "the thickness of an ear lobe." The shape should be roughly oblong, rather than perfectly round.

Grease 2 baking trays with a little vegetable oil and place 2 pieces of dough on each. Divide the meat topping into 4 and spread all over the surface. Bake the breads 2 at a time for 10 to 12 minutes, until the topping is cooked through and the corners attractively brown — but the bread should not become too crisp.

to serve Scatter the onion rings, sumac (if you have it) and parsley over the surface, squeeze half a lemon over each bread, roll up — and eat.

Making gözleme, Tlos, southern Turkey

Bakery, Damascus, Syria

Gözleme

If *lahmacun* and *pide* are the Turkish pizzas, then this is the Turkish pancake. This cheese-filled village bread is traditionally made over a slightly rounded griddle on a wood fire. I find an upturned wok a good — if slightly unorthodox — substitute; you could also use the bottom of a large, non-stick skillet or a proper griddle. Making the bread is an art that very few of us acquire; you should only make this recipe if you can buy the right bread already made (as Turkish housewives do). (See page 54.)

makes 2   *3 1/4oz feta cheese;*
6 tablespoons ricotta cheese;
several sprigs of fresh thyme;
freshly ground black pepper; paprika; unsalted butter;
2 sheets of dogan yufka *made especially for the purpose*
  (note: it is sold in packs of 3 and is a huge round when
  unfurled — buying 3 is a good idea in case you spoil
  the first one);
a good handful of fresh parsley, leaves roughly chopped

method   Place the upturned wok, skillet or griddle over medium heat. Make the filling by mashing together the cheeses and the stripped leaves of the thyme. Add a little pepper and paprika to taste.

Rub a little butter over the cooking surface and lay over a sheet of the *yufka* at once. Sprinkle half the filling, together with half the parsley, over the surface and fold in the edges to form a package. Cook for a couple of minutes, until the filling starts to melt, then carefully turn over (it is easiest to do this using another plate to slide the *yufka* onto). Cook again for a minute or so until lightly charred. Cut into 4 pieces — and eat.

a sweet tooth

The presentation of the fruit bowl at a feast was the sign that the

meal was drawing to its close. After the various meze, rich pilafs

and delicately spiced meat and vegetable stews, a plate of cherries on ice or slices of sweet pink

watermelon was all that was needed to round off the meal. And if fresh fruit was not in season, dried

fruits could take their place, simmered in syrups scented with flower waters, sweetened with honey,

stuffed with nuts. But the Ottoman Empire was also famous for its sweets and pastries — Turkish

delight and baklava to name but two. These were pleasures to be enjoyed with a cup of coffee,

midmorning or midafternoon, quite separately from the main meal. Many of the pastries were given

salacious names, such as "lady's navel" or "beauty's lips"; others referred jokingly to the wealthy of the empire, as in "the Grand Vizier's fingers" (short and fat). There was *aşure* or Noah's pudding, a

concoction of wheat, legumes and rice cooked with dried fruits, said to be Noah's invention from the

food left in the Ark. Most exotic of all was a pudding made from chicken breasts, sweetened with sugar

and cooked in milk to acquire its unique, almost rubbery, texture.

Such puddings are still eaten in Turkey today. Many of these delicacies lay in the domain of the

muhallebeçi, the maker of milk puddings, although Turkish delight and pastries also had their own

specialists. Istanbul still boasts stores devoted to each of these particular skills and just as the French

buy in their patisserie there is no shame in turning to the masters of their art. For cooking at home,

here are some simpler — but no less alluring — recipes.

Stuffed apricots in syrup

*7oz dried apricots (not the presoaked variety);
juice of 1/2 lemon; 4 tablespoons white sugar;
1 tablespoon orange-flower water; freshly whipped cream;
finely crushed green pistachios (unsalted)*

method   Cover the apricots with warm water and leave to soak, either overnight or for at least 5 hours.

Make the remains of the soaking water up to 1 cup. Add the lemon juice and a few strips of the lemon zest, the sugar and orange-flower water. Place in a shallow pan in which all the apricots will fit in one layer and bring the syrup to a boil, stirring continuously. Boil hard for 2 minutes then reduce to a simmer and carefully add the apricots. Let simmer, uncovered, for 20 minutes, gently turning the fruit halfway through.

Leave the apricots to cool in the syrup. Just before you serve them, use a sharp knife to slit each apricot in half lengthwise, leaving them still attached on one side. Slide a scant teaspoonful of the whipped cream into the resulting pouch. Place the fruit on the serving plate and dribble some of the syrup over. Scatter with the crushed pistachios just before serving.

Walnut-stuffed figs

One sassy stallholder in Istanbul's Egyptian Bazaar describes these as "Turkish Viagra."

*1 cup weak black tea; 7oz dried figs (about 12) — they
    should be fat and juicy, the surface of the fruit
    neither broken nor crushed, and with visible stems;
3 tablespoons honey; juice of 1/2 lemon;
5 fresh bay leaves; walnut halves (with skin)*

method   Pour the tea, still warm, over the figs and leave to soak, either overnight or for at least 5 hours.

Make the soaking liquid back up to 1 cup with some water. Pour into a shallow pan in which all the figs will fit snugly in one layer and add the honey and the lemon juice, together with the bay leaves. Bring the syrup to a boil, stirring continuously, and boil hard for 2 minutes then reduce to a simmer. Carefully add the figs, stem side up. Let simmer, uncovered, for 20 minutes, basting the figs with the syrup occasionally. Let cool in the syrup.

When the figs are cool enough to handle, use a sharp knife to make a slit across the side of the stem of each one. Stuff a walnut piece into this. Place the figs in a serving dish and pour the honey and tea syrup over, together with the bay leaves. The figs will keep, and even improve, for a day or two before serving.

Almond milk pudding with rosewater syrup

This exquisite pudding, with its delicate almond flavor, perfumed syrup and jewellike studding of pomegranate seeds and pistachios, truly shows off the art of the *muhalle-beçi*. Except that it is surprisingly easy to make.

makes 6 to 8 puddings depending upon the size of the molds
for the pudding   *3 cups whole milk;*
11/4 cups finely ground blanched almonds;
2 tablespoons rice flour;
heaped 1/2 cup white sugar;
for the syrup   *1 cup water;*
1/2 cup white sugar; 1 tablespoon rosewater
to decorate   *1 tablespoon green pistachios*
    (unsalted), finely sliced;
seeds of 1/2 pomegranate

method   To make the puddings, first warm the milk. Pour 1 ladle or cupful into the ground almonds and stir well until you have a porridgy paste. Pour another ladle or cupful into the rice flour and stir until completely smooth — make sure there are not any lumps.

Return the milk to low heat and stir in the sugar, followed by the almond and the rice-flour pastes. Cook, stirring continuously, for 15 to 20 minutes, until you have a smooth and very thick cream. Spoon into small molds (I like to use round ones and find glass easiest to turn out). Let cool.

Meanwhile, make the syrup. Simply mix together the water and sugar and bring to a boil, stirring to dissolve the sugar. Boil hard for 2 minutes then take off the heat. Stir in the rosewater and let cool.

When the puddings are cool enough to handle, turn them out and pour a little of the rosewater syrup over and around each. Sprinkle with the sliced pistachio and scatter around the pomegranate seeds. Let stand for an hour or so before serving.

Rice pudding

Sold in little individual earthenware bowls, rice pudding is one of the most popular carry-out puddings throughout the eastern Mediterranean region. If you can get hold of mastic, it provides a much-admired chewy consistency, while the saffron adds its unique honeyed flavor and color. The pudding is eaten cold.

1 cup short-grain pudding rice
a pinch of sea salt; 41/2 cups whole milk;
11/2 cups white sugar; 1/2 teaspoon saffron strands;
3 crystals of mastic (optional)

method   Bring 11/2 cups water to a boil, together with the pinch of salt, and then, using a heavy-bottomed pan, boil the rice until small holes appear in the surface and all the water has evaporated — this should take 5 to 6 minutes.

Now turn the heat down to low and add the milk, sugar, saffron and mastic if you have it. Heat the oven to 400°F. Cook the rice, stirring all the time, for 20 minutes or so, until the mixture is thick. Pour into 4 earthenware bowls, preferably wide ones, and transfer to the heated oven. Cook for another 15 minutes, until the surface is nicely brown. Let cool before serving.

Baklava

This famous Turkish pastry is, in fact, of Christian origins — its original name of *baki-halva* translates as "Lenten sweet" and originally the baklava had forty sheets of pastry dough, one for each of the days of Lent. Armenian Christians are believed to have first brought it to Constantinople, where it was quickly taken over by the seraglio to become the favorite pastry of the court. In typically excessive fashion the sultans' chefs vied to produce ever more elaborate and expensive versions, resulting in the rich and sticky pastry with which we are familiar today — studded with nuts, oozing butter and laden with sugar syrup. You only need the smallest lozenge to complement a cup of coffee.

serves 8 to 10   *1 cup white sugar;*
4 tablespoons honey;
juice of 1/2 lemon; 2 cups water;
2 tablespoons rosewater;
2 sticks unsalted butter;
1 teaspoon ground cinnamon;
scant 1 cup each of shelled, blanched walnuts,
* pistachios and almonds, roughly chopped;*
12oz package of yufka *(see p54) or, failing that,*
* phyllo pastry dough, rectangular in shape*

method   Put the sugar, honey, lemon juice and water in a pan and bring to a boil. Boil, uncovered, for 6 to 7 minutes, stirring regularly, until the syrup is thick enough to coat the back of a spoon. Stir in the rosewater and let cool.

Heat the oven to 350°F. Melt the butter and skim off the scum that rises to the surface. Mix the cinnamon into the nuts.

Lay a sheet of dough on a baking tray and paint the upper surface with melted butter. Repeat with another 3 sheets then sprinkle a third of the nut and cinnamon mixture over. Cover with 4 more sheets of dough, brushing each time with butter, then add another third of the nuts. Repeat the process to use up the remaining nuts and dough, brushing the surface of the last piece especially liberally with butter.

With a sharp knife, make diagonal crosses across the surface of the baklava, so you have lozenge shapes.

Bake the baklava for 30 minutes in the heated oven. Then lower the temperature to 300°F. Bake for 45 minutes longer, until the surface is nicely brown. Pour the cool syrup over, making sure plenty gets down between the cracks. Let cool thoroughly before serving.

Dried fruit and nut salad

Ottoman cuisine was highly seasonal and the habit of preserving fruit in the fall remains strong throughout the region. Not for them the underripe, overrefrigerated fruit shipped from some far-off land that so many of us tolerate (if not expect) of our supermarkets. Instead, perfectly ripe figs, grapes and apricots are dried under the sun, distilling their essential sugars. These treats can be munched on throughout the day, but for a winter pudding they are reconstituted in perfumed water and mixed with nuts. This is a Lebanese version — in Turkey the fruits are typically stewed, but I prefer the chewy texture that long maceration gives. If you don't have the time, however, soak the fruits overnight and then stew them in a little water before adding the perfume and nuts.

12oz dried apricots; 8oz dried figs;
11/3 cups seedless raisins; heaped 1/2 cup sugar;
2 tablespoons rosewater or orange-flower water;
scant 1 cup blanched almonds or a mixture of
  almonds and pistachio nuts

Place the dried fruits in a large bowl and sprinkle the sugar and the scented water over. Pour in enough water to just cover the fruits and leave in a warm place for 48 hours. Add the nuts and chill well before serving.

variation You might want to add walnuts and pine nuts instead of almonds and pistachios.

Sweet-seller, Aleppo, Syria

Sour cherry bread pudding

A Turkish version of English summer pudding, given its deep red hue from the sour cherries, which have been first made into jam and juice.

12oz jar of sour cherry preserve (you can also
  use sour cherry jam);
10 slices white bread, crusts removed; sour cherry juice

method Melt the cherry preserve in a saucepan over low heat, stirring all the time. Lightly toast the slices of bread. In a glass bowl, build a pudding, starting with a layer of bread, followed by a little of the melted cherry preserve and a few tablespoons cherry juice. Repeat the process 3 or 4 times, adding just sufficient cherry juice to cover the bread. Weigh down with a plate and refrigerate for at least 12 hours before serving. In Turkey, this pudding is traditionally served with *kaymak*, thick cream made from buffalo milk; you can use freshly whipped cream.

Rose-petal ice

The Ottoman's first capital was in Bursa, across the Sea of Marmaris from Constantinople and on the slopes of the snow-capped Mount Uludağ. In spring, ice was brought down from the peak to make cooling sherbets, scented with perfumes such as rose- or orange-flower water. This pretty pink rose-petal ice comes from that tradition.

21/4 cups water; heaped 1/2 cup white sugar;
juice of 1 lemon; 2 tablespoons rosewater;
12oz jar of rose-petal jam

method Mix together the water and sugar and bring to a boil. Turn down to an active simmer and let bubble for 5 minutes, until you have a light syrup. Let cool for 15 minutes or so, then stir in the lemon juice, rosewater and the rose-petal jam.

Pour into a wide container suitable for the freezer and freeze for 4 hours, whisking every hour to break up the ice crystals. You can freeze it for longer, but make sure you take it out of the freezer 20 minutes before serving and whisk it well just before spooning into glass bowls.

note You can find rose-petal jam in most Turkish, Greek and Middle Eastern food stores.

Bottled rosewater

Turkish delight and coffee

The favorite sweet of the ladies of the harem, among whom voluptuousness was a much-admired virtue, its name in Turkish (*rahat lokum*) means giving rest to the throat. Far from the sickly sweet and virulently colored versions available commercially, true Turkish delight is chewy in consistency and delicate in flavor.

The best Turkish delight in the world is reputed to come from the shop of Haçi Bekir, started in Istanbul more than two hundred years ago and still going strong. Haçi Bekir opened its doors in 1777 and today the shop retains its old-fashioned feel, with its wood paneling and vast hunks of halva in the window.

opposite *Turkish coffee and Turkish delight* **below** *candy stalls at bazaars in Istanbul, Turkey (note the sign for "Turkish Viagra" — see p118)*

A proudly displayed certificate announces that their Turkish delight won a gold medal at the Brussels 1897 International Exhibition. Tens of varieties of delight are on offer, from those studded with pistachio or almonds to pale pink cubes scented with rosewater. Judging from the steady stream of customers, Turkish delight remains as popular in Istanbul today as it was at the time of the sultans.

Coffee arrived in the Ottoman Empire

from Yemen in the mid-sixteenth century; the Turks still say if they have to wait for their coffee it must be "coming from Yemen." The first public coffee house was opened in Constantinople by two Syrians in 1554, a hundred years before coffeehouses reached Paris and London. It was apparently the Turkish ambassador to Paris who first introduced the French to the delights of coffee, and an Armenian from the Ottoman Empire set up the first Parisian coffeehouse in the seventeenth century. Coffee soon became the drink of choice, despite one Turk at the time describing it as "the black enemy of sleep and copulation." In the capital of Constantinople coffeehouses were renowned as political talking shops and in 1712 officials even tried to have them closed down to prevent additional unrest; although no sooner was one group closed than another set sprang up. Today in Istanbul coffeehouses remain a social focus, at least for the men — at any time of day you can find them sitting over their cups of coffee lamenting the past, hatching plots for the future, doing business deals and criticizing the government.

Turkish coffee is served short, strong and sweet. It is traditionally made, with a certain amount of ceremony, in a small copper pot with a long handle. First water and sugar are added and brought to a boil, then a generous amount of coffee is stirred in and the thick liquid brought back to the boil not once but four times. The coffee is poured, still fizzing, into small cups and true masters of the art always seem to get the quantities exactly right.

Café, Syria

preserving the harvest

Winters can be harsh in this region, whether on the high Anatolian plain or in the mountains of the Balkans. Fall sees furious preserving activity, to make sure that even when there is snow on the ground there will be vegetables and fruit to eat. But if preserving and pickling was born through necessity, many of the dishes have become delicacies in their own right. There are the long, crisp green peppers without which no Turk would consider a meze table complete; the lurid pink turnips stained with beet juice that are a Lebanese favorite; and the red peppers, at their best dried in the sun, which will flavor pilafs through the long, cold winter. And as a sweet end to the meal, a mouthful of fruit preserved in sugar syrup or even a teaspoon of the concentrated grape juice known as *pekmez*.

opposite *red peppers drying, Dalyan, Turkey* **above** *mixed pickles*

Making pekmez, *Yassiçal, Turkey*

Candied pumpkin

This sweet preserve is a particular favorite among Turkish children, who, as a treat, suck on the candied yellow strips as they make their way to school.

2lbs pumpkin; 11/4 cups white sugar;
2/3 cup water

method   Remove the skin and seeds of the pumpkin and cut the flesh into thin strips.

Mix together the sugar and water and, in a large, wide pan, bring slowly to a boil, stirring all the time so the sugar dissolves. Add the pumpkin strips, preferably in one layer. Simmer gently in the syrup for 45 minutes, stirring regularly to prevent the strips of pumpkin from sticking together. At the end of cooking the pumpkin should be very soft and translucent.

Arrange the strips of pumpkin on a sheet of parchment paper on an oven tray, making sure none of them are touching. Heat the oven to its lowest possible setting. Leave the pumpkin slices in the oven for about 12 hours. Let cool — the pumpkin will become crisp.

variation   Instead of drying the slices of pumpkin in the oven, allow them to cool in the syrup and add a tablespoon of rosewater. Serve in small glass bowls, topped with thick, freshly whipped cream and walnuts.

Preserves stall, Thessaly, Greece

Spoon sweets These little fruits preserved in sugar syrup acquired their name because they are quite literally

served from a spoon at the end of the meal. Only a mouthful or two is needed to provide that shot of sugar and sweet fruit.

Favorites include green figs, cherries, apricots and quince, but I have also had spoon sweets made from cherry tomatoes and

even small pickling eggplants. Spoon sweets are best bought from specialist shops, unless you are a keen maker of jams and

preserves, but overleaf are two easy recipes for fruit in syrup.

Quinces in syrup

In the fall, vast piles of golden yellow, down-covered quince can be seen in Turkish markets, their delicate scent wafting in the air. In the Britain of several centuries ago, a bowl of two or three quinces was used to perfume the kitchen, in the same way as oranges. But we seem to have lost the habit of the quince, perhaps because it must be cooked before eating. Happily, the quince remains a favorite fruit in the East, whether cooked with meat (see recipe page 97), made into jam or gently stewed in syrup.

2 large quinces, about 13/4lbs in total;
juice of 1 lemon; 4 cloves; 1 cup white sugar;
21/4 cups water; 1 green apple

method Peel the quinces and cut them into quarters lengthwise. With a sharp knife, remove the hard core, but preserve 7 or 8 of the seeds. Place the quinces in a large, heavy pan with a lid — they should fit snugly in a single layer. Quickly pour the lemon juice over to prevent them from discoloring.

Add the cloves, the reserved quince seeds, the sugar and the water to the pan. Peel the apple and grate the flesh coarsely over the quince. Cover the pan and place over low heat. Cook for 1 to 11/4 hours, occasionally basting the quince with the syrup. The exact cooking time will depend upon the ripeness of the fruit. When ready, they will be soft to the touch, but still holding their shape, and a delicate salmon pink in color.

Carefully lift the quince out of the pan and place in a serving dish. Turn the heat under the pan up to medium and simmer the syrup for 10 minutes or so, uncovered, stirring regularly. Your aim is to reduce it to a syrupy, almost jellylike consistency. Pour this syrup over the quince (you can pick out the seeds and cloves, but I just leave them in) and let cool a little before serving. These are especially delicious (and translucently beautiful) served just warm with freshly whipped cream.

Figs in syrup

This is a good treatment for figs doomed never to reach full-blown ripeness due to overchilling.

1lb fresh, slightly underripe figs;
juice of 2 large lemons;
21/2 cups white sugar; a stick of cinnamon;
sterilized glass jars

method Wash and dry the figs well. Cut them into quarters if they are small, eighths if they are plumper. Pour over the lemon juice and let stand 10 minutes.

Place the figs and lemon juice in a heavy, nonreactive (not metallic) pan. Add the sugar and cinnamon stick and place the pan over low heat. Simmer for 15 minutes, shaking the pan occasionally, rather than stirring it, which will break up the figs. Let the mixture cool and then bottle, syrup and all, in the sterilized glass jars.

above from left *highland pastures, Dukagjin, Albania; harvesting apples, El Mali, Turkey; threshing sesame, Patara, Turkey* **opposite** *Safranbolu, Turkey*

A visit to a hill village A perilous road led up an apparently sheer

cliff face and I was beginning to regret my decision to visit the mountain village

of Yassiçal, high above the Turkish riverside town of Amasya. But my guide Hüseyin

was so pleased to be going home that to express any qualms felt churlish.

And then suddenly the road opened out onto a beautiful upland plateau and I

knew that coming here was the right thing to have done. As we arrived in town,

we were greeted by a band of old men walking along playing their instruments.

There was a wedding planned for the next day and they were warming up.

A combination of the wedding and the fine fall weather meant the village was full of activity. First stop was the main house of the village, where in one corner of the courtyard some dozen women sat by an open fire rolling and baking the flat breads that would be needed at the wedding feast, the wood regularly replenished from a stack borne by a donkey. I was taken to admire the fine dowry of beautifully embroidered headscarves and delicate table lace.

And then we wandered around the streets, Hüseyin stopping regularly to greet members of his extended family, all of whom seemed to be cooking in the street. One was stirring her pot of beets for sugar syrup, another chopping onions for salad, a third pounding nigella seeds. We admired the carpets set out in the weak sun for fall airing, tasted stuffed grape leaves cooked with pieces of goat meat on the bone, sipped strong tea. It was a delight.

opposite *Safranbolu, Turkey* **below from left** *corn drying, Anatolia; weighing onions, Safranbolu; musicians, Yassiçal, Turkey*

Market at Burdur, Turkey

Pickled green peppers

The long, thin green peppers beloved of the Turks and Greeks alike are found in vast piles in the markets in fall, ready for pickling. Brined in vinegar to preserve their crisp texture and slightly sharp flavor for the winter months, no meze table is complete without them. Eaten just as they are, be warned that they can be hot — as in fiery. If you don't want them to burn your mouth, don't add the chili peppers.

2lbs green peppers, stems trimmed;
4 tablespoons coarse sea salt;
3 cups white-wine or grape vinegar;
6 black peppercorns; 1 tablespoon white sugar;
2 or 3 small dried red chili peppers (optional);
1 large Mason jar, sterilized

method Rinse the peppers and place them in a large earthenware crock or china bowl (it is important that the material is nonreactive — so do not use metal). Sprinkle over 3 tablespoons of the salt and add just enough warm water to barely cover the peppers. Let stand in the brine for at least 6 hours; overnight is best.

Mix the remaining salt into the vinegar, together with the peppercorns and sugar. Bring to a boil and allow to simmer for 5 minutes. Meanwhile, drain the peppers and pat dry. Pack them, stems upright, into the Mason jar, adding the chili peppers if you are using them. Pour in the hot vinegar, top up with boiling water and let cool before sealing.

Store in a cool and dark place for at least 3 weeks before using. The pickled peppers will keep for several months unopened. Once opened, they should be kept in the refrigerator and used within a few weeks.

variation The same method can be used for mixed pickles. A typical combination would be long green peppers, cabbage leaves (preferably from a *lahano* cabbage), sliced carrots and a few whole peeled cloves of garlic.

Marinated olives

One happy fall day I drove along the shores of Lake Iznik in Turkey as the local farmers were bringing in the olive harvest. The setting sun sparkled on the blue waters, glimpsed through the venerable olive groves that stretch down to the lake shore. Beneath the gnarled trees, nets were spread out to catch the fruit; wooden ladders were propped against the trunk, and on them perched young women in their distinctive floral patterned dresses, shaking the branches. On the road there was a traffic jam of tractors and trailers, dodging the occasional donkey dragging the long, handmade ladders. When I reached the nearby village, I discovered the reason for all this activity: the buyer from the local olive oil cooperative had arrived.

But not all the olives are pressed to make the sweet, fruity olive oil that this area is famous for producing. Later, in the nearby Bursa market, I found piles of shiny, green fruit to be preserved at home. I don't go that far, but I do like to dress my olives up. This recipe for olives with pomegranates, red pepper flakes and capers comes from Turkey's Edremit province, but is very similar to a version of marinated olives that I enjoyed in Lebanon's Bekaa Valley.

8oz Kalamata olives;
1 heaping tablespoon capers, rinsed;
1 tablespoon concentrated pomegranate juice;
1 tablespoon grape vinegar;
2 tablespoons extra-virgin olive oil; red pepper flakes;
1 small fresh pomegranate or 1/2 large one

method Place the Kalamata olives in an earthenware dish and add the capers. Beat together the pomegranate syrup, vinegar and oil and pour over the olives and capers. Add a generous sprinkling of red pepper flakes and let marinate, preferably overnight.

Before serving, remove the seeds of the pomegranate, making sure you discard any white pith, and add them to the olives and capers.

Index

Note: Page numbers in *italics* indicate an illustration

Picture Acknowledgments The publisher would like to thank the following photographers and picture agencies for their kind permission to reproduce the photographs in this book:

4 left Jeremy Horner/Hutchison Picture Library; 4 right Trip; 5 John Brunton; 7 Christine Osborne Pictures; 9 Michael Jenner/Robert Harding; 11 Pietro Cenini/Panos Pictures; 14 Sarah Woodward; 15 Caroline Penn/Impact; 16 left C. Bowman/Axiom Photographic Agency; 16 right Sarah Woodward; 17 John Brunton; 19 Sarah Woodward; 20 A. Ghazzal/Trip; 23-24 G. Simpson; 27 Sarah Woodward; 28 John Brunton; 31 Robert Frerck/Odyssey/Chicago/Robert Harding; 32 Robert Francis/Hutchison Picture Library; 34 Sarah Woodward; 37 Nigel Lea-Jones/Anthony Blake Photo Library; 41 & 47 Sarah Woodward; 51 Ian Wallace/Food & Travel magazine; 52 Guy Moberly/Anthony Blake Photo Library; 56-57 Peter Rayner/Axiom Photographic Agency; 59 Nick Tapsell/ffotograff; 60 Sarah Woodward; 68 Sarah Woodward; 69 Alan Keohane/Impact; 70-71 Sarah Woodward; 72 Robert Frerck/Odyssey/Chicago/Robert Harding; 78 Dexter Hodges/Axiom Photographic Agency; 79 Sarah Woodward; 81 Patrick Syder/Anthony Blake Photo Library; 86 Peter Cassidy/Food & Travel magazine; 87 Andy Stewart/Anthony Blake Photo Library; 87 above Sarah Woodward; 87 below Maddie Thornhill/Narratives; 88 Sarah Woodward; 89 Trip; 95 Sarah Woodward; 97 Elizabeth Whiting & Associates; 100 John Brunton; 101 Chris Stowers/Panos Pictures; 102 Nick Tapsell/ffotograff; 107 Fred Friberg/Robert Harding; 108 P. Rayner/Axiom Photographic Agency; 110 left Sarah Woodward; 110 right John Brunton; 111 Jeremy Horner/Hutchison Picture Library; 113 Sarah Woodward; 114 Tony Waltham/Robert Harding; 116 Guy Marks/Axiom Photographic Agency; 123 Alan Keohane/Impact; 124 Patrick Syder/Christine Osborne Pictures; 127 D. Shaw/Axiom Photographic Agency; 127 right Christine Osborne Pictures; 129 Patrick Syder/Anthony Blake Photo Library; 130 Michael Short/Robert Harding; 132 Sarah Woodward; 133 James Morris/Axiom Photographic Agency; 136 left Rhodri Jones/Panos Pictures; 136-139 Sarah Woodward; 140 C. Bradley/Axiom Photographic Agency

Every effort has been made to trace the copyright holders and we apologize in advance for any unintentional omission, and would be pleased to insert the appropriate acknowledgment in any subsequent editions.

Author's Acknowledgments With thanks to:
The Turkish Tourist Office and especially Joanna Marsh; Turkish Airlines; Ustalik Belgesi for showing me true Turkish delight in Safranbolu; Rosemary Barron for her kind introductions; Tania and Serge Hochar of Château Musar for the best meal I had in Lebanon; Hüseyin from the Ilk Pansiyon in Amasya, for taking us to his home village, Yassıçal; Mr Kanounji of the Yildizlar restaurant, Beirut, for fabulous meze; Elizabeth Payne for humoring me in southern Turkey; John Scott of Cornucopia for his very helpful guidance; Michel and Figen Tesson of Les Jardins de Levissi, Kayaköy; the chef of the Restaurant Âsitâne, Karayi Oteli, Istanbul; the cook at the Hotel Chbat, Bcharrée, for showing me how to make *kibbeh nayé*.

Most importantly, Jonathan Gregson, who first took me to Turkey on our honeymoon and has been traveling and tasting with me ever since.